StLouis
Chefs' Recipes
Volume 2

With our print publications and digital products—*St. Louis Magazine*, *St. Louis At Home*, *St. Louis Family*, *St. Louis Chefs' Recipes*, Hello GoodBuy!, and stlmag.com—SLM Media Group, a locally owned and operated company, has built a desirable audience within the St. Louis metropolitan area, through award-winning editorial and design; paid, targeted circulation; signature events; and an educated and affluent readership.

Our informative, beautiful publications were created to serve as the local authority on what is so great about the Gateway City. We provide our readers—both monthly through our print publications and daily through our website—with useful, current information that helps them make the most out of living in St. Louis. Through our pages, St. Louisans can connect with their city in a whole new way.

Copy Editors: Anne Cori, Alicia Kellogg, Anna Ross, Margaret Schneider
Food Photography and Styling by Greg Rannells
Portrait Photography by Kevin A. Roberts

This book was produced by SLM Media Group.
1600 S. Brentwood, Ste. 550
St. Louis, MO 63144
314-918-3000 | stlmag.com

For distribution information, call 314-918-3006.

A portion of the proceeds from the sale of this cookbook will go to support Operation Food Search, the St. Louis region's largest distributor of free food for the hungry.

INTRODUCTION

One success begets another, and who would have thought that our first venture into the culinary world of cookbooks would have been such a hit? Published last fall, *St. Louis Chefs' Recipes* quickly sold out, required additional printings, and raised nearly $5,000 for Operation Food Search.

With those kinds of results, we stepped back into the batter's box to swing for another home run with Volume II. This time around, more than 100 local chefs and mixologists contributed some of their most-prized recipes—from Companion's incomparable clam chowder to Cardwell's at the Plaza's savory cheese torte, from Pastaria's *cacio e pepe* to Trattoria Marcella's legendary lobster risotto—and so much more.

From breakfast and lunch to cocktails and dinner, we have it covered. From downtown St. Louis to as far away as Clarksville's Overlook Farms, we have found something that will appeal to every palate. And as with our first cookbook, we asked chefs for doable dishes—created with standard measurements. If a *sous-vide* cooker was involved, we requested a second entry. We don't have that equipment; we suspect you don't either.

For the second time around, we are again proud to state that we will be donating a portion of sales to Operation Food Search, the volunteer-based organization that connects no-longer-saleable food with people in need.

As we write this, new restaurants are opening, and existing restaurants are shuttering. It's hard to keep ahead of the curve, but we have done our best to get the newest chefs on the scene to contribute their favorite recipes. And if some of the restaurants listed are no longer operating, you will have recipes to remember them by. It is our hope that some of these dishes will become family favorites.

Enjoy every bite.

Christy   *Mye*

Christy Marshall, Editor-in-Chief, *St. Louis At Home* and *St. Louis Family*
George Mahe, Dining Editor, *St. Louis Magazine*

OPERATION FOOD SEARCH

Founded in 1981, this volunteer-based organization was formed by concerned civic and community leaders who created a green solution to rescue food that is no longer saleable, yet is safe, nutritious, and edible, then get it onto the plates of hungry people in St. Louis and 30 surrounding Missouri and Illinois counties. Operation Food Search procures perishable and nonperishable food from grocers and the restaurant and catering industries, food manufacturers, and distributors for its network of community partners, as well as food pantries, soup kitchens, and shelters to feed hundreds of thousands of low-income and impoverished families and individuals, of whom one-third are children.

In addition to food distribution, Operation Food Search programs and initiatives include:

COOKING MATTERS
A robust, culinary-based nutrition education program

OPERATION BACKPACK
A weekend feeding program that serves children who are the most at risk for hunger and food insecurity

NO KID HUNGRY
A nationwide anti-hunger advocacy campaign

Operation Food Search is privately funded by individuals, corporations, and foundations; by the faith community; and through special events. Less than 2 percent of revenue is used for administration and fundraising, which means that 98 percent goes directly to program services.

OPERATION
FOOD
SEARCH

OPERATIONFOODSEARCH.ORG

CONTENTS

RECIPES FROM ST. LOUIS' TOP CHEFS, VOLUME 2

Breakfast & Brunch

BALABAN'S EGGS MADISON

D. SCOTT PHILLIPS, BALABAN'S WINE CELLAR & TAPAS BAR

SERVES 6

Water

1/2 cup distilled vinegar

12 large eggs

6 plain English muffins, split

1 tablespoon unsalted butter, melted

12 pieces smoked salmon

Hollandaise sauce (see recipe)

1 tablespoon red onion, thinly sliced

1 tablespoon capers

Pour enough water into 2 large skillets to reach a depth of about 3 inches, and divide the vinegar between them. Bring both skillets to a gentle simmer over medium heat. Crack an egg into a cup and carefully slide the cup into the hot poaching liquid. Quickly repeat with all of the eggs. Poach the eggs, turning them occasionally with a spoon until the whites are firm or to the desired degree of doneness, about 3 to 5 minutes. Using a slotted spoon, remove the eggs and transfer them to a kitchen towel. Lightly dab the eggs with the towel to remove any excess water.

Warm six plates. Brush the English-muffin halves with melted butter and toast them. Place two muffin halves on each of the plates. Top each half with a piece of smoked salmon, and set an egg on top. Spoon the hollandaise sauce over the eggs and garnish them with the thinly sliced red onion and capers. Serve this dish immediately.

HOLLANDAISE SAUCE

YIELDS ABOUT 1 1/2 CUPS

1 1/3 cup unsalted butter

Water

2 large egg yolks

2 tablespoons cold water

1 tablespoon freshly squeezed lemon juice, strained, plus more as needed

1 teaspoon kosher salt

Freshly ground white pepper or cayenne pepper

In a medium-size pan, completely melt the butter over medium-low heat. Remove it from the heat and set it aside for 5 minutes. Skim and discard the white foam that rises to the surface of the butter. Carefully ladle or pour the clear golden butter into a container with a pouring spout. Take care not to add the milky solids and watery liquid at the bottom of the saucepan. Set the clarified butter aside in a warm spot.

Pour enough water into a medium saucepan to reach a depth of about 2 inches. Bring the water to a gentle simmer over medium heat. In a medium-size heatproof bowl, combine the egg yolks and the 2 tablespoons of cold water. Whisk until the yolks are light and frothy. Place the bowl over the saucepan of simmering water and whisk the yolks constantly and vigorously until they're thickened and light, about 3 to 4 minutes. (If the yolks begin to scramble or the mixture is cooking very quickly or gets too hot, remove the bowl from the saucepan and whisk it to cool the yolks.)

Remove the bowl from the saucepan and whisk the sauce for 30 seconds to cool it slightly. Remove the saucepan from the heat and place the bowl back over the water. Slowly drizzle the clarified butter into the eggs while whisking constantly. Whisk in the lemon juice, salt, and a pinch of white pepper or cayenne pepper to taste. (If the sauce is very thick, add a few drops of warm water to adjust the consistency so it is creamy and light.) Serve the sauce immediately, or keep it in a small bowl set over warm—not hot—water for up to 30 minutes, or in a warmed Thermos for up to an hour.

BOURBON BUNS

SIMONE FAURE, CHOUQUETTE

SERVES 12

Vegetable oil

2 cups all-purpose flour

2 tablespoons white sugar

4 teaspoons baking powder

1 teaspoon salt

$1/4$ cup butter

1 cup milk

$1/3$ cup butter

1 cup packed brown sugar

3 teaspoons ground cinnamon

2 tablespoons bourbon

3 cups pecans, toasted

Bourbon-vanilla glaze (see recipe)

Preheat the oven to 350 degrees. Prepare one 12-cup muffin pan by oiling the bottom and sides. In a large bowl, combine the flour, sugar, baking powder, and salt. Cut in the $1/4$ cup of butter until the mixture resembles coarse crumbs. Make a well in the middle of the mixture and pour in the milk. Mix it until it's blended in. Turn the dough out onto a floured surface and knead it eight to 10 times. Roll the dough out into a rectangle 12 inches long and 1 inch thick; trim off any uneven edges.

Mix together the $1/3$ cup of butter, brown sugar, bourbon, and ground cinnamon until it's light and creamy. Divide the toasted pecans between the muf-

fin cups, then drop small amounts of the butter-sugar mixture into the greased muffin pan. Spread the remainder of the butter-sugar mixture evenly over the rectangular dough.

Starting at the short end, roll the dough into a log, jellyroll-style, and cut it into 12 pieces. Place one piece in each cup of the muffin pan. Bake the buns for 20 to 25 minutes. Remove the pan from the oven, let the buns sit in the pan for 10 minutes, then invert it to remove them. While the buns are slightly warm, cover them with bourbon-vanilla glaze.

BOURBON-VANILLA GLAZE

$1 1/2$ cups confectioners' sugar

$2 1/2$ teaspoons milk

$1/8$ teaspoon salt

$1/4$ teaspoon vanilla extract

1 tablespoon bourbon

1 teaspoon butter

Mix together the sugar, milk, salt, vanilla extract, bourbon, and butter until it's light and creamy.

CHEDDAR-CHIVE BUTTERMILK BISCUITS WITH CHICKEN GRAVY

DAVID KIRKLAND, CAFÉ OSAGE

SERVES 8

16 cheddar-chive biscuits (see recipe)

Chicken gravy (see recipe)

Micro greens or chives

CHEDDAR-CHIVE BISCUITS

2 cups all-purpose flour, plus extra for rolling

1 tablespoon baking powder

1/4 teaspoon baking soda

3/4 teaspoon salt

1/2 cup butter, chilled, or 1/2 cup shortening

1 1/4 cups buttermilk

1/2 cup shredded cheddar

1/4 cup chopped chives

Preheat the oven to 450 degrees. In a large mixing bowl, whisk together the flour, baking powder, baking soda, and salt. Working quickly, using your fingertips, rub the butter or shortening into the dry ingredients until the mixture looks like crumbs.

Make a well in the center of the mixture and pour in 1 cup of the buttermilk. Add the cheese and chives. Stir the mixture just until the dough comes together; it will be very sticky. Turn the dough onto a floured surface. Dust the top of the dough with flour and gently fold it over on itself five or six times.

Form the dough into a 1-inch-thick round. Cut out biscuits with a floured 2-inch-wide cutter, being sure to push straight down through the dough. Place the biscuits on a lined baking sheet so that they just touch. Re-form the scrap dough, working it as little as possible, and continue cutting out biscuits.

Use the remaining buttermilk to brush the tops of the biscuits. Bake the biscuits until they're tall, light, and golden on top, or approximately 15 to 20 minutes. This recipe should make 16 biscuits.

CHICKEN GRAVY

1 quart milk

1 teaspoon nutmeg

1/2 cup butter

1/2 cup flour

2 teaspoons celery salt

2 teaspoons white pepper

1 tablespoon and 1 teaspoon sea salt

2 tablespoons olive oil

3 large leeks, thinly sliced

4 cups crimini mushrooms, thinly sliced

6 chicken breasts

Preheat the oven to 350 degrees. In a 4-quart pot, heat the milk and nutmeg, making sure that the milk doesn't boil. In a separate pan, melt the butter and add the flour to make a light roux. When the roux is well mixed, add the celery salt, white pepper, and sea salt. Then whisk in the warmed milk and nutmeg. Keep the gravy on low heat until it thickens.

Add 1 tablespoon of the olive oil to a sauté pan over medium-high heat. Cook the sliced mushrooms and leeks until they are soft and tender. Do not overcook them. Add them to the gravy.

Coat the chicken breasts with the remaining tablespoon of olive oil and bake them in a pan for about 1 hour at 350 degrees. Once the chicken is done, let it cool, then cut it into cubes. Add the chicken to the gravy.

To serve: In each of eight rimmed soup bowls, ladle chicken gravy over two split cheddar-chive biscuits. Garnish with the micro greens or chives.

COFFEE COFFEE CAKE WITH CRÈME-FRAÎCHE ICE CREAM

JOSH GALLIANO, THE LIBERTINE

SERVES 8

COFFEE CAKE

12 tablespoons unsalted butter, softened

2 cups sugar

4 teaspoons baking powder

1 teaspoon salt

1 tablespoon cocoa powder

1 tablespoon instant espresso powder

1 ¼ cups milk

3 cups all-purpose flour

3 egg whites

Nonstick baking spray

Coffee-cake topping (see recipe)

Preheat the oven to 375 degrees. Place the softened butter and sugar in the bowl of a stand mixer. Use the paddle attachment to beat the sugar and butter together on medium speed until it's pale yellow in color and fluffy in volume. Add the baking powder, salt, cocoa powder, and espresso powder to the stand mixer and combine them on low speed.

Add the milk and all-purpose flour to the stand mixer in alternating batches on low speed. In a separate mixing bowl, beat the egg whites with a whisk until they form stiff peaks. This simple meringue may take 5 minutes of whisking, so have a helper nearby who can take over when your arm gets tired. Add the beaten egg whites into the stand mixer and combine them into the batter.

Spray a 13- by 9-inch baking pan with nonstick baking spray, then pour in the batter. Break up pieces of the coffee-cake topping over the batter. Place the baking pan in the oven and bake the cake for about 45 minutes, or until a cake tester comes out of the cake clean. You may have to rotate the pan in your oven while it bakes; check every 10 to 15 minutes to make sure the coffee cake is baking as evenly as possible.

COFFEE-CAKE TOPPING

12 tablespoons unsalted butter, softened

¾ cup all-purpose flour

1 ½ cups light brown sugar

2 tablespoons cinnamon

6 tablespoons cacao nibs

Thoroughly combine all of the ingredients in a mixing bowl.

GRAHAM-CRACKER TUILE

¼ cup sugar

¼ cup water

1 cup graham-cracker crumbs

Salt

To make a simple syrup, combine the sugar and water in a saucepan and heat it until the sugar is dissolved. Let it cool. Mix together ⅓ cup of the syrup with the graham-cracker crumbs and a pinch of salt to form the tuile dough.

Preheat the oven to 350 degrees. Spray two pieces of parchment paper with nonstick baking spray. Place the tuile dough between the two pieces of parchment and roll it out. Place it on a tray and bake it for 15 to 20 minutes. When it's crisp, remove it from the oven and let it cool to room temperature.

CRÈME-FRAÎCHE ICE CREAM

1 quart milk

1 ¼ cups sugar

12 egg yolks

Salt

1 ¼ cups crème fraîche

To make the ice-cream mixture, heat the milk in a pot to about 170 degrees. Separately, mix together the sugar, egg yolks, and a pinch of salt. Whisk some of the heated milk into the egg mixture. Then combine both mixtures in the pot. Return it to the stove over medium heat while constantly stirring, until it again reaches 170 degrees.

Remove the pot from the heat. Whisk the crème fraîche into the ice-cream mixture, then pass it through a chinois or fine strainer. Cool the mixture in the refrigerator.

CONTINUED ON PG. 16

Baked Eggs in Hash-Brown Nests

TIM BRENNAN, CRAVINGS

SERVES 6 (2 PER PERSON)

3 large russet potatoes

½ yellow onion

Butter or nonstick
baking spray

2 cups fresh arugula

¼ cup yellow onion,
finely chopped

1 tablespoon Dijon
mustard

Salt and pepper

¼ cup olive oil

6 ounces creamy goat
cheese

1 dozen large eggs

Preheat the oven to 400 degrees. Boil the potatoes whole and unpeeled until they're fork-tender, about 25 minutes. Let them cool and remove the skins. (This may be done a day in advance.)

Once the potatoes are completely cool, grate them on the largest opening of a box grater. Grate the half onion on the box grater as well, and mix it with the potato. Spray or butter a 12-cup muffin pan. Press about ¼ cup of the potato-onion mixture into the bottom and sides of the tin, forming an opening in the center.

Bake these for 8 to 12 minutes, or until the top edges are golden brown. Remove them from the oven and let them cool completely. (This may be done one day in advance.)

Place the arugula, ¼ cup finely chopped onion, mustard, a pinch of salt, and a pinch of pepper in the bowl of a food processor and purée it. With the machine running, gradually add the olive oil. Scrape down the bowl and process the purée again until it's smooth. (This may be made a day in advance.)

Preheat the oven to 400 degrees. Place a generous tablespoon of the arugula purée and a tablespoon of goat cheese in the bottom of each potato-lined muffin pan. Crack an egg into a small bowl and carefully pour it into the prepared muffin pan. Repeat this process to fill each muffin cup. Bake the pan for 8 to 12 minutes, or until the egg whites are set and the yolks are still runny.

Process the cold ice-cream mixture in an ice-cream machine according to the manufacturer's instructions.

To serve: Tear off two large chunks of coffee cake and place them on a plate. Layer some broken pieces of the graham-cracker tuile in between the pieces of coffee cake. Place a scoop of crème-fraîche ice cream next to the coffee cake. To help keep the ice cream in place, you may want to place it on top of graham-cracker crumbs.

CRAB-AND-GRAPEFRUIT AMBROSIA WITH TUILES

TRENT THRUN, CORONADO BALLROOM AND STEVEN BECKER FINE DINING

SERVES 15

19 sheets of gelatin

Ice water

7 cups grapefruit juice

1 3/4 cups grenadine

2 pounds canned pasteurized lump
   crabmeat, chilled

2 cups whipped cream

1/4 cup chives

1 1/2 teaspoons salt

1/2 teaspoon black pepper

1/2 lemon, juiced

Tuiles (see recipe)

To make the grapefruit gelée, first soak the gelatin sheets in ice water for about 15 minutes. Combine the grapefruit juice and grenadine. Heat 2 cups of the juice-grenadine mixture in a medium saucepot. Remove the liquid from the heat and lightly stir it, but do not whisk. Drain the gelatin sheets and stir them into the warm sauce until they're dissolved. Immediately add the remaining juice

mixture and fill 15 champagne flutes. Place the glasses at an angle and refrigerate them to set the gelatin.

To make the crab salad, drain the crabmeat until it is dry. Fold in the whipped cream, chives, salt, pepper, and lemon juice.

TUILES

1 cup sugar

4 tablespoons butter, softened

1/2 cup all-purpose flour

2 grapefruits, zested

Preheat the oven to 300 degrees. Mix the sugar and butter in a mixer until it's smooth. Mix in the flour and grapefruit zest. Spread this batter onto a Silpat silicone liner in 15 very thin rounds. Bake the tuiles until they're golden, about 10 minutes. Carefully remove the tuiles from the Silpat and reserve.

To serve: Pipe the crab salad on top of the grapefruit gelée, then place a tuile on top of the salad as a garnish.

DUCK-CONFIT CREPES

**AARON TEITELBAUM,
HERBIE'S VINTAGE 72**

SERVES 4

1/4 cup duck confit (see recipe)

3 tablespoons heavy cream

2 tablespoons Chambord liqueur

Kosher salt

Black pepper

2 tablespoons habanero jack cheese

4 crepes (see recipe)

2 tablespoons truffle honey

Chambord reduction sauce (see recipe)

DUCK CONFIT

- ¼ cup kosher salt
- 2 tablespoons fresh thyme
- 1 tablespoon dried juniper berries
- 2 garlic cloves, peeled
- 2 tablespoons black peppercorns, crushed
- 2 Mulard or Muscovy duck legs
- 8 cups oil, preferably duck fat, though vegetable oil is acceptable

At least two days in advance, mix the kosher salt, thyme, juniper berries, garlic, and pepper in a food processor until it's a loose paste. Coat all areas of the duck legs with this mixture, cover them, and let them sit in the refrigerator for at least 24 hours.

One day in advance, wash the seasoning off of the duck legs, place them in a Dutch oven, and cover them in the oil or duck fat. Cook the duck at 275 degrees until it's tender, about 3 hours. You should only see a few bubbles every so often. Let the duck cool in the oil overnight. The day of serving, pick the meat off of the bones. Duck confit can be made up to a week in advance.

CHAMBORD REDUCTION SAUCE

- ½ cup Chambord, reduced by half

Pour the Chambord into a small saucepan. Over low heat, cook it slowly until the liquid is reduced by half and to a consistency of syrup.

CREPES

- ½ cup all-purpose flour
- 1 egg
- ¼ cup milk
- ¼ cup water
- ⅛ teaspoon salt
- 1 tablespoon butter, melted
- Vegetable oil

In a large mixing bowl, whisk together the flour and egg. Gradually whisk in the milk and water. Add the salt and melted butter. Beat the batter until it's smooth.

Over medium-high heat, heat a lightly oiled griddle or frying pan. Pour ¼ cup of batter onto the griddle for each crepe. Using a circular motion, tilt the pan until the batter coats it evenly. Cook each crepe about 2 minutes, or until the bottom is light brown. Loosen it with a spatula and flip it over to cook the other side.

To serve: Add the duck confit to a hot pan with the cream, the Chambord, and kosher salt and black pepper to taste. Melt in the cheese, then place the mixture in the crepe, fold it over, and plate it. Drizzle the truffle honey and Chambord reduction over the top of each crepe.

FRITTATA WITH POTATO, BACON, AND CARAMELIZED ONION

RUSSELL PING, RUSSELL'S CAFÉ & BAKERY AND RUSSELL'S ON MACKLIND

SERVES 6 TO 8

- ¼ pound bacon, chopped
- 2 Yukon Gold potatoes, peeled and diced
- 1 large onion, diced
- 2 or 3 garlic cloves, peeled and minced
- 1 dozen eggs
- ¾ cup beer
- ⅓ cup buttermilk
- ¼ teaspoon cumin
- Kosher salt and pepper

Start the bacon in a cold oven-safe pan, then heat it to medium, and the fat will render out faster. Once the

CONTINUED ON PG. 20

**NY VONGSALY,
BAR LES FRÈRES,
BOBO NOODLE HOUSE,
AND I FRATELLINI**

What is your favorite cooking tip? Be sure your utensils are ready and your ingredients are measured and portioned before you ever pick up a pan or turn on the heat.

What is the one ingredient that should be in the pantry? High-quality cooking oil.

Gruyère Soufflés

NY VONGSALY

BAR LES FRÈRES, BOBO NOODLE HOUSE, AND I FRATELLINI

SERVES 6

Nonstick baking spray

4 tablespoons butter

½ cup flour

2 cups heavy cream, warmed

4 egg yolks

1 ½ cups Gruyère cheese, grated

1 teaspoon salt

½ teaspoon cayenne pepper

2 tablespoons fresh chives, chopped

6 egg whites

Preheat the oven to 425 degrees. Lightly grease six ramekins with nonstick baking spray and place them on a rimmed sheet pan. Melt the butter over low heat. Add the flour and stir until it's well combined. Remove this mixture from the heat and gradually add the warmed cream. Stir in the egg yolks and return the mixture to medium heat. Bring it to a boil. Add the cheese, salt, cayenne pepper, and chives, and stir until the cheese is melted. Remove the mixture from the heat.

Whip the egg whites until soft peaks form. Slowly fold the egg whites into the mixture. Pour the mixture into ramekins up to three-quarters full. Bake the soufflés for 20 minutes, or until they're puffed. Serve them immediately.

bacon is crispy, remove it from the pan. Toss the diced potatoes and onion into the hot bacon fat. Cook the potatoes and onion until the potatoes are brown and the onion is caramelized. Once the onion begins to caramelize, add the minced garlic and continue to sauté. Pour in about half of a bottle of beer and cover the pan for about 5 minutes, which steams the potatoes so they are cooked through. (Guess you will have to drink the other half of the beer—darn.)

Preheat the oven to 400 degrees. Crack all of the eggs into a bowl and whisk in the buttermilk, the cooked bacon, the cumin, and kosher salt and pepper to taste. Pour this egg mixture into the pan with the potatoes, onion, and garlic. Place the entire pan in the oven and bake it for about 15 minutes, or until the egg is cooked through. Once the frittata is cooked, pull it out of the oven and immediately flip it onto a plate or cutting board.

Note: Brunch should have elements of breakfast and lunch. Ping likes to serve a simple salad with this frittata to cut the heaviness of all of the eggs and bacon.

GOUGÈRES FILLED WITH SMOKY-SPICY EGG SALAD

STEPHEN TROUVERE, BAILEYS' CHOCOLATE BAR, BRIDGE, AND ROOSTER

MAKES 50 GOUGÈRES

1 cup water

$1/2$ cup butter

1 cup all-purpose flour

4 ounces Emmentaler cheese, shredded

1 teaspoon salt

4 large eggs

Smoky-spicy egg salad (see recipe)

3 sprigs fresh tarragon

Bring the water and butter to a simmer. Stir in the flour all at once, then beat it with a spatula or spoon over low heat for 1 minute, or until the batter is smooth and ropy. Add the cheese and salt. Beat the batter until the cheese is melted into it. Transfer the batter to a mixer with a paddle attachment. Beat the batter on medium, adding the eggs one at a time until it's smooth and sticky. Pour the batter into a pastry bag with a plain or fluted tip. Pipe $1 1/2$-inch-diameter rings onto parchment, building each up into a short cone.

Bake the gougères at 375 degrees for about 30 minutes, or until they're golden and crisp on the outside and hollow and dry on the inside. Let them cool completely, then split them with a knife and fill them with egg salad. Add a leaf or two of tarragon to each plate for a garnish.

SMOKY-SPICY EGG SALAD

6 eggs

1 cup sour cream

2 shallots, minced

2 teaspoons smoked paprika

1 teaspoon sherry vinegar

$1/2$ teaspoon sugar

$1/4$ teaspoon cayenne pepper

1 teaspoon salt

Hard-boil the eggs, about 10 minutes, then chill them in an ice bath. Whisk together the sour cream, shallots, smoked paprika, sherry vinegar, sugar, cayenne pepper, and salt to make the sauce. Peel and chop the eggs and place them in a clean bowl. Add dollops of sauce to the eggs until you achieve the desired level of sauciness. Taste and add salt if necessary.

MOTHER'S DAY QUICHE

ADAM LAMBAY,
CHAUMETTE VINEYARDS & WINERY

SERVES 4

2 cups heavy cream

8 egg yolks

6 eggs

1 tablespoon salt

1/2 teaspoon ground black pepper

1 sheet puff pastry

Butter

1 cup fresh spinach, blanched and chopped

1 cup Gruyère, shredded

1/2 cup Parmesan, grated

Preheat the oven to 300 degrees. Whisk together the cream, egg yolks, eggs, salt, and pepper in a bowl. Cut the puff pastry into quarters and roll it out slightly. Gently press the dough into 4 buttered ramekins or a 9-inch pie pan. Arrange the spinach on top of the puff pastry and top it with the cheese. Pour the filling over the top of the spinach and cheese. Bake the quiche for 30 to 40 minutes.

PANCAKES TOPPED WITH CHEVRE-HONEY MOUSSE AND CITRUS

STEPHEN TROUVERE,
BAILEYS' CHOCOLATE BAR,
BRIDGE, AND ROOSTER

SERVES 8

16 ounces goat cheese

1/2 cup honey

1 lemon, zested

2 lemon rinds, thinly julienned

2 orange rinds, thinly julienned

2 lime rinds, thinly julienned

4 cups cold water

2 cups plus 2 tablespoons sugar

1 1/2 cups all-purpose flour

1 teaspoon baking powder

1/2 teaspoon salt

1 1/2 cups whole milk

2 eggs

4 tablespoons butter, melted

Butter, vegetable oil, or nonstick cooking spray

To make the mousse, beat the goat cheese, honey, and lemon zest together until it's smooth and fluffy. Set it aside to use at room temperature.

To make the candied citrus topping, place the pieces of lemon, orange, and lime rind in a pot with the cold water and 2 cups of sugar. Simmer the liquid on low until the rind is very tender and 75 percent of the liquid is gone. Strain out the rind and toss it with 2 tablespoons of sugar. Store it in an airtight container.

To make the pancake batter, whisk together the 2 tablespoons of sugar, flour, baking powder, and salt. In a separate bowl, whisk together the milk, eggs, and melted butter. Pour the wet ingredients into the dry ones, mixing gently until they're combined. Lumps are okay; do not overmix.

To form each pancake, pour about 1/4 cup of the batter onto a hot, greased griddle on medium-low heat. Cook it until bubbles rise to the surface of the pancake and the lower half is firm. Flip it and cook it just until the center is springy to the touch. Hold the pancakes warm in the oven until serving.

To serve: Layer the warm pancakes with a generous smear of the mousse, then top them with the candied citrus and another dollop of mousse.

Heavenly French Toast
With Blueberry Compote

HELEN FLETCHER, THE ARDENT COOK AND TONY'S

MAKES 18 SLICES

CORNBREAD

1 cup plus 2 tablespoons cornmeal

1 1/3 cups all-purpose flour

1/2 cup sugar

1 tablespoon plus 2 teaspoons baking powder

1/2 teaspoon salt

1 egg

1 1/3 cups milk

5 tablespoons unsalted butter, melted

FRENCH TOAST

Butter

4 eggs

1 cup whole or 2 percent milk

1 tablespoon vanilla

3 tablespoons sugar

1/2 teaspoon nutmeg

Preheat the oven to 350 degrees (or 325 degrees if you're using a dark or glass pan). Grease or spray an 8- by 2-inch square pan and set it aside.

Place the cornmeal in a food processor and process it for 3 to 4 minutes to grind it as finely as possible. In a large bowl, combine the cornmeal with the flour, sugar, baking powder, and salt.

In a small bowl, lightly beat the egg and whisk in the milk and butter. Pour this over the dry ingredients and whisk to combine them. Pour the batter into the prepared pan and bake it for 45 to 50 minutes, until it's golden brown and a tester comes out clean.

The cornbread may be frozen if desired; if so, thaw it completely before slicing it.

Slice the cornbread vertically. Trim both outside edges. Slice each half of the cornbread into 3/4–inch slices.

Place a pat of butter into a nonstick pan and melt it, but do not let it brown. In a bowl, whisk the eggs until they're completely blended. Add the milk, vanilla, sugar, and nutmeg (more sugar and nutmeg can be added to taste), and whisk to combine them. Pour the mixture into a shallow bowl or pan for dipping. Dip both sides of each piece of bread into the mixture. Place the piece in the hot pan. Cook it until it's golden, flip it over, and cook the other side.

Serve the French toast with warm blueberry compote. If you want to hold the French toast, heat the oven to 150 degrees. Place the toast on a baking sheet, lightly covered with foil, and set it in the oven.

BLUEBERRY COMPOTE

1/2 cup water

1/2 cup sugar

1 12-ounce bag frozen blueberries

Place the water and sugar in a saucepan. Whisk it well. Add 2/3 of the blueberries and bring the liquid to a boil. Lower it to a simmer and cook it until a few drops of the liquid are somewhat thickened when poured from a spoon. Remove the saucepan from the heat. Purée the mixture in a blender or food processor, then add the remaining blueberries. The compote can be made a week ahead if desired. Heat it before serving.

SAVORY GOAT-CHEESE TORTES

BILL CARDWELL, CARDWELL'S AT THE PLAZA AND BC'S KITCHEN

SERVES 12

1 cup cornmeal

1/2 cup butter, melted

Butter or nonstick baking spray

1 pound cream cheese, softened

1/3 cup heavy cream

1 1/3 tablespoons fresh thyme

1 2/3 tablespoon fresh chives

1 onion, roasted and chopped

Salt and pepper

1 pound goat cheese

4 eggs

Hot water

To make the crust, preheat the oven to 325 degrees. Combine the cornmeal with the melted butter until the mixture resembles wet sand and just holds together when squeezed. Grease or spray two springform pans and spread this mixture on the bottom and sides of each. Bake this crust until it's lightly browned, about 10 minutes.

Turn the oven down to 280 degrees. To make the filling, use a stand mixer's paddle attachment to mix the cream cheese until it's free of lumps. Add the cream, thyme, chives, onion, and salt and pepper to taste and mix well. Add the goat cheese and mix until it's just combined. Add the eggs and mix until they're just combined.

Wrap the outside of the two springform pans with foil. Divide the batter into the pans. Place the pans into a roasting pan. Fill the roasting pan with 1 inch of hot water. Bake the tortes for approximately 40 minutes, being careful not to overbake them.

SOUTHERN-STYLE SPICY FRENCH TOAST WITH MASCARPONE AND BACON JAM

JODIE FERGUSON, TABLE THREE

SERVES 8

2 eggs

2 egg yolks

2 cups milk

1 cup heavy cream

1/4 cup sugar

1 tablespoon cinnamon

1 teaspoon cayenne pepper

1 teaspoon vanilla extract

1 loaf brioche, Pullman loaf, or Italian or French bread

Butter

Mascarpone

Bacon jam (see recipe)

Preheat the oven to 350 degrees. Whisk together the eggs, egg yolks, milk, cream, sugar, cinnamon, cayenne pepper (can add more or less to taste), and vanilla until it's smooth. Cut the bread into thick slices, soak each slice thoroughly in the egg mixture, and transfer the slices to a parchment-lined baking sheet. Bake the French toast until it's golden brown, or 8 to 10 minutes. Let it cool.

Melt butter in a sauté pan over medium heat and place each slice of baked French toast in it to brown. Top the browned slices with mascarpone and bacon jam.

Note: Ferguson serves this with slow-cooked grits. It reminds her of home, but with a twist.

BACON JAM

1 pound bacon, cut into 1-inch pieces

1 pound yellow onions, diced small

1 garlic clove, peeled and minced

½ cup brewed coffee

¼ cup apple-cider vinegar

⅓ cup brown sugar

¼ cup maple syrup

Render the bacon in a pan over medium heat and cook it until it's crisp. Pour off the rendered bacon fat. Add the onions and garlic to the pan and sauté them over medium-heat until they're translucent. Add the coffee, apple-cider vinegar, brown sugar, and maple syrup and cook to reduce the liquid. As the mixture cools, it should resemble jam.

WINSLOW'S HOME ROLLED OMELET

CARY McDOWELL, FORMERLY WITH WINSLOW'S HOME

SERVES 8 TO 10

Butter, vegetable oil, or nonstick baking spray

12 large pasteurized, cage-free eggs

1 cup whole milk

¼ cup unbleached all-purpose flour

Salt and pepper

1 4-ounce can roasted, peeled, preserved peppers

1 bag baby spinach, preferably organic

3 ounces fontina cheese, shredded

Mixed salad greens and/or breakfast potatoes

Preheat the oven to 350 degrees. Lightly lubricate a rimmed half-sheet baking pan (13 by 18 inches) and line it with a piece of parchment paper. Be sure that the paper

rises above the pan's edges on all sides so that you may pour liquid inside without it leaking.

Mix the eggs, the milk, the flour, and salt and pepper to taste, making sure there are no lumps, and pour the liquid into the prepared pan. Gently mix in some of the peppers, making sure they are evenly dispersed. Add ⅔ of the raw spinach on top of the liquid mix (this will bake in).

Carefully place the pan into the preheated oven and bake until the egg sets up throughout, 8 to 10 minutes. When the egg is just set, remove the pan from the oven and top the omelet with the remaining spinach and all of the cheese. Return the omelet to the oven for 2 minutes more.

Remove the omelet from the oven and let it stand no more than 5 minutes, just long enough to cool so you can roll it. Carefully roll it, using the excess paper as a tool, into a tight, snug roll, much like a jellyroll. Let it stand at least 10 minutes, so the roll sets up.

Remove the paper and cut the roll into round slices. Serve it with a small tuft of mixed salad greens and/or breakfast potatoes.

Note: This technique is extremely versatile and often used at Winslow's Home for breakfast or brunch. The omelet can be easily prepared in advance and reheated gently before serving.

The ingredients can be varied by the season. Seasonal flavor combinations served at Winslow's Home have included asparagus–goat cheese; Ozark shiitake with Swiss-style cheese; red chard–and–smoked bacon; pulled chicken with butternut squash; hot smoked salmon, arugula, and feta; and oxtail with spring onions and Gouda.

Soups, Salads & Sandwiches

BACON-POTATO SALAD

DON TADLOCK, KEMOLL'S

SERVES 6

1/2 cup uncooked bacon, finely minced

1 1/2 cups red potato, diced

2 hard-boiled eggs, finely minced

1/4 cup white onion, finely minced

1/4 cup celery, finely minced

1/4 cup red bell pepper, finely minced

1 tablespoon garlic, peeled and chopped

1 tablespoon parsley, chopped

1 1/2 cups sour cream

1/2 cup grated Parmesan cheese

1 1/2 cups mayonnaise

1 tablespoon Worcestershire sauce

1/2 tablespoon white vinegar

1 1/2 tablespoons Dijon mustard

1/2 teaspoon white pepper

1 1/2 teaspoons salt

1 tablespoon granulated sugar

1 teaspoon lemon juice

1 pinch ground red pepper

1 pinch dried sweet basil

1 pinch dried oregano

1 cup extra-virgin olive oil

Iceberg or romaine lettuce

In a sauté pan, render the minced bacon and add the diced potato. Sauté it until the bacon is slightly crisp. Place the bacon and potato into the refrigerator to cool. Once they're cool, combine them with the minced eggs, onion, celery, and red bell pepper in a large mixing bowl.

To make the dressing, in another bowl, combine the garlic, parsley, sour cream, Parmesan, mayonnaise, Worcestershire sauce, vinegar, Dijon mustard, white pepper, salt, sugar, lemon juice, and spices. Mix these items together until they're creamy, then slowly whisk in the olive oil to get a great consistency. Toss the potato mix with the dressing. Serve the dressing with a wedge of iceberg or romaine lettuce.

CLEVELAND-HEATH BEET SALAD

JENNY CLEVELAND AND ERIC HEATH, CLEVELAND-HEATH

SERVES 6 TO 10

3/4 cup feta cheese

1/4 cup shallots, minced

1 cup green onions, sliced

Kosher or sea salt

Sherry vinaigrette (see recipe)

Beets (see recipe)

Faro (see recipe)

Chimichurri (see recipe)

1/3 cup Marcona almonds, toasted and
   roughly chopped

SHERRY VINAIGRETTE

2 cups extra-virgin olive oil

1 teaspoon salt

1/2 cup sherry vinegar

Whisk the extra-virgin olive oil and salt into the sherry vinegar until they're emulsified.

BEETS

6 large beets or 12 small beets

1 head garlic

1 cup sherry vinegar (or cider vinegar)

2 bay leaves

⅓ cup salt

Water

Place the beets, garlic, sherry vinegar, bay leaves, and salt in a medium-size pot or saucepan. Add enough water to cover the beets and bring it to a boil. Reduce the liquid to a simmer and cook until the beets are tender all the way through. Larger beets take up to 2 hours, smaller ones about an hour. Then remove the beets from the water and let them cool. Once they're cool enough to handle, take a paper towel and peel the beets by wiping off the skin. (A trick to knowing your beets are cooked all the way is that the skin will simply wipe off, without much work.) Once the beets are peeled, quarter them or cut them into bite-size pieces and set them aside.

FARO

1 cup faro

1 teaspoon salt

2 ½ cups water

Place the faro, salt, and water in a small pot. Bring the water to a boil, then reduce it to a simmer. Cook until the faro is tender all the way through.

CHIMICHURRI

2 cups cilantro leaves

1 cup mint leaves

1 cup flat-leaf parsley leaves

¼ cup sherry vinegar

1 tablespoon garlic, chopped

1 teaspoon salt

¼ cup extra-virgin olive oil

Water or lemon juice (optional)

Place the cilantro, mint, parsley, sherry vinegar, garlic, and

salt in a blender or food processor. Purée the mixture until it's smooth. With the machine running, drizzle in the olive oil. If the mixture is too dry for the blender, add a little water or lemon juice to loosen it up a bit.

To serve: In a large mixing bowl, combine the feta, shallots, and green onions, plus salt to taste. Dress the mixture with just enough sherry vinaigrette to coat it. Fold in the beets and faro. Spread the chimichurri on salad plates. Top each plate with a pile of beet salad, and garnish it with almonds.

BRUSSELS-SPROUT SLAW

KEVIN TAYLOR, BISTRO 1130

SERVES 4

1 pound Brussels sprouts

Dressing (see recipe)

2 ounces Kerrygold Dubliner cheese, grated

2 tablespoons almonds, toasted and crushed

2 radishes, sliced thin

6 grape tomatoes, halved

1 sprig fresh marjoram, chopped

1 sprig fresh rosemary, chopped

Cut off the root end of each sprout, then shave it on a mandoline or in a food processor.

DRESSING

3 tablespoons extra-virgin olive oil

1 tablespoon white truffle–infused olive oil

1 ½ tablespoons lemon juice

Salt and pepper to taste

Whisk the oils into the lemon juice and season well.

To serve: Toss the sprouts with the dressing, then top them with the Dubliner cheese, almonds, radishes, and tomatoes. Garnish with the marjoram and rosemary.

GREEN BEAN–AND–ANCHOVY SALAD WITH ORANGE-AND-FENNEL PICKLED EGGS

MATHIS STITT, VERITAS GATEWAY TO FOOD AND WINE

SERVES 6

6 farm-fresh hard-boiled eggs, room temperature

1 cup packed brown sugar

1 cup apple-cider vinegar

1 cup orange juice

2 teaspoons ground turmeric

1/2 teaspoon salt

5 bay leaves

1/2 teaspoon chili (or red pepper) flakes

1/2 teaspoon dried fennel seed

4 juniper berries (optional)

1 cup fresh fennel bulbs, thinly sliced

1 cup fresh orange, sliced 1/4 inch thick

Salted water

Ice water

1 1/2 pounds fresh green beans

1/4 cup crème fraîche

Salt

12 Ortiz skinless anchovy fillets packed in oil, or the best-quality available

To make the orange-and-fennel pickled eggs, peel the eggs and set them aside.

Combine the brown sugar, vinegar, orange juice, turmeric, and salt in a stainless-steel pot. Bring the liquid to a simmer.

Place the bay leaves, chili flakes, and fennel seed into a quart-size canning jar. Optionally, add the juniper berries. Layer the peeled eggs, sliced fennel bulbs, and orange slices on top of the dry ingredients in the jar.

Pour the simmering liquid into the jar to cover the eggs. Allow the jar to cool on the counter. After it's cool, cover it with a lid and refrigerate it for at least 48 hours. The pickled eggs will keep, refrigerated, for at least two weeks.

To make the salad, bring a large pot of salted water to a boil and prepare a large bowl of ice water for an ice bath. Trim the stems from the green beans, if needed, and drop the beans into the rapidly boiling water.

When the water comes back to a boil, transfer the beans to the ice bath with a slotted spoon or tongs. Once the beans are cool, remove them from the bath and set them aside.

Drain the pickled eggs, reserving the pickling liquid and vegetables. Quarter the eggs and set them aside. To make the dressing, mix the crème fraîche with a teaspoon or two of the pickling liquid, adding salt to taste.

To serve: Separate about a half cup of the pickled fennel bulbs into a mixing bowl. Add the green beans and enough of the dressing to thinly coat the vegetables. Toss the mixture and divide it onto six individual dishes or one large serving plate. Top the salad with the pickled eggs and anchovies.

GRILLED SALAD

SCOTT THOMAS, GRILLIN' FOOLS

SERVES 4 TO 6

2 heads romaine lettuce

2 tablespoons olive oil

2 teaspoons granulated garlic or garlic powder

Coarse salt and freshly cracked pepper

1/2 cup Romano, Asiago, or Parmesan cheese, grated

Remove the outer leaves of each head of romaine. Rinse the heads under cold water. Slice each head down the center lengthwise. With each half flat-side-down, drizzle it with olive oil, and dust it with the granulated garlic, salt, and black pepper. Flip it over and repeat.

Prepare the grill for high-heat grilling. Place the half-heads of romaine flat-side-down over the coals. Once the flat side of each has a nice blackened char, after about 2 to 3 minutes, depending on the heat of the grill, flip it over and sear half of the curved side. After another 2 to 3 minutes, rotate each half-head to char the other half of the curved side.

Remove any leaves that come loose during the cooking process. Once the flat side and the curved side of each half-head are charred, remove it from the heat, place it on a platter, and sprinkle grated cheese on the lettuce.

Serve immediately.

Note: Do not eat the bottom 2 inches or so at the base of each half-head. Romaine lettuce is known to collect dirt and grit. The only reason the base isn't cut off is because the lettuce would fall apart like confetti on the grill without it.

ROASTED GOLDEN BEET SALAD

CHRIS DiMERCURIO, ELEMENT

SERVES 2

2 ounces soft goat cheese

1/2 cup heavy cream

1/2 bunch parsley, stemmed and roughly chopped

1 teaspoon fresh thyme leaves

1 tablespoon shallots, minced

1 clove garlic, peeled and minced

1 tablespoon sherry vinegar

2 tablespoons olive oil

Kosher salt

Fresh ground pepper

4 small golden beets, roasted, peeled, and diced

1 bunch mint, stemmed and roughly chopped

1 1/2 cups micro greens or spring mix

1/4 cup pistachios, roasted and crushed

Whip the goat cheese with the heavy cream until it's smooth, then fold in the chopped parsley and thyme leaves.

To prepare the vinaigrette, combine the sherry vinegar with the garlic and shallots and whisk in the olive oil. Season with kosher salt and fresh ground pepper to taste.

In a bowl, toss the roasted beets, fresh mint, and micro greens with the vinaigrette. Smear half of the prepared goat cheese onto each plate with the back of a spoon. Top it with the salad mixture and a sprinkle of crushed pistachios.

Summer Melon Salad

MELISSA LEE, THE RITZ-CARLTON, ST. LOUIS

SERVES 5

---

2 tablespoons lemon
   vinaigrette (see recipe)

½ cup watermelon, 1-inch
   dice

½ cup honeydew melon,
   1-inch dice

½ cup Charentais melon,
   1-inch dice

3 hearts of palm, cut into
   1-inch-long pieces

1 ounce goat cheese

4 teardrop tomatoes,
   sliced

Micro arugula

1 teaspoon balsamic
   reduction (see recipe)

LEMON VINAIGRETTE

1 teaspoon Dijon mustard

1 ½ teaspoons lemon zest, finely grated

Coarse salt and freshly ground pepper

6 tablespoons extra-virgin olive oil

Combine the Dijon mustard and lemon zest. Add salt and pepper to taste. Whisk in the olive oil to incorporate.

BALSAMIC REDUCTION

½ cup balsamic vinegar

Bring the balsamic vinegar to a boil in a saucepan. Cook until it's reduced by half.

To serve: Toss the watermelon in a teaspoon of the vinaigrette and arrange it on each plate. Arrange the honeydew and Charentais melon pieces around it, and add the hearts of palm pieces, goat cheese, and tomatoes. Garnish with micro arugula. Spoon the remaining dressing around each plate, then drizzle the balsamic reduction along the outside. Spoon bits of the goat cheese onto the fruit.

ROASTED HALIBUT WITH BLOOD ORANGE–FENNEL SALAD

REX HALE, BASSO, THE MARKET AT THE CHESHIRE, THE RESTAURANT AT THE CHESHIRE, AND THREE SIXTY

SERVES 4

1 cup blood-orange segments

1/4 cup blood-orange juice

1 fennel bulb, trimmed

2 tablespoons red onion, julienned

2 tablespoons red bell pepper, julienned

2 tablespoons Kalamata olives, chopped

1 teaspoon salt

1/8 teaspoon red pepper flakes

1/4 cup extra-virgin olive oil

4 6-ounce halibut pieces

1/4 teaspoon ground black pepper

Fresh pea shoots or watercress

Preheat the oven to 375 degrees. In a small bowl, combine the blood-orange segments and juice. Halve the fennel bulb lengthwise, slice it thinly, and add it to the orange pieces. Add the red onion, the red bell pepper, the Kalamata olives, 1/2 teaspoon of the salt, the red pepper flakes, and the olive oil. Stir to combine.

Meanwhile, place the fish on a roasting dish. Sprinkle it with the remaining 1/2 teaspoon of salt and the black pepper and bake it for 10 to 12 minutes, depending on its thickness. Gently transfer the fish to a serving plate. Top it with the blood orange–fennel salad, garnish it with fresh pea shoots or watercress, and serve it immediately.

ROOT-VEGETABLE SALAD

RACHEL OBERMEYER, PRIME 1000

SERVES 4

1 carrot, peeled and cut into 3 inch-long pieces

1 parsnip, peeled and cut into 3 inch-long pieces

1 fennel bulb

2 radishes

Vinaigrette (see recipe)

2 cups baby arugula

2 tablespoons *pepitas* (pumpkin seeds), toasted

Granola (see recipe)

Using a mandoline, carefully shave paper-thin slices of the carrot, parsnip, fennel bulb, and radishes. Reserve the slices in ice water.

VINAIGRETTE

1 tablespoon *pepitas* (pumpkin seeds), toasted

1 tablespoon fennel seed

1/2 cup white-wine vinegar

1 tablespoon honey

Soybean oil

Salt

Place the *pepitas* and fennel seed in a blender and pulse till they're roughly ground. Add the vinegar and honey and blend at low speed. Slowly drizzle in the soybean oil till it's emulsified. Add salt to taste.

GRANOLA

2 tablespoons honey

1 tablespoon maple syrup

1 teaspoon brown sugar

1/8 teaspoon red chili flakes

1 cup puffed-rice cereal

3/4 cup oats

Salt

Preheat the oven to 250 degrees. In a pan, heat the honey, maple syrup, brown sugar, and red chili flakes. Pour the resulting syrup over the puffed rice and oats. Salt to taste. Spread the mix evenly over a sheet tray. Bake the granola until it's toasted and crispy, approximately 30 minutes. Let it cool on the sheet tray.

To serve: Once the vinaigrette is ready, drain the vegetable slices and toss them with the vinaigrette and arugula. Season the mix with salt and pepper, then arrange it on plates. Top the salads with toasted *pepitas* and crumbled granola.

SALMON TATAKI AND SHAVED SALAD

CHRIS LEE, RIVER CITY CASINO

SERVES 8

7 ounces boneless, skinless fresh salmon fillets

Freshly ground black pepper

Jalapeño vinaigrette (see recipe)

Shaved salad (see recipe)

Heat a nonstick skillet until it's medium hot. Season the salmon fillets with black pepper and sear them for 5 seconds on each side. Make sure the outside of each fillet is completely seared. Immediately plunge the fillets into ice water to stop the cooking process, then drain and pat them dry with paper towels. Refrigerate.

JALAPEÑO VINAIGRETTE

1 small jalapeño pepper, chopped

1 teaspoon salt

1 teaspoon garlic, peeled and chopped

6 1/2 tablespoons rice vinegar

1/2 cup extra-virgin olive oil

Place the jalapeño, salt, garlic, and vinegar in a blender and purée until the mixture is smooth. With the machine running, drizzle in the oil to form an emulsion.

SHAVED SALAD

1 carrot, peeled

1 zucchini

1 yellow squash

2 small turnips, peeled

4 red radishes

2 beets, peeled

With a mandoline, thinly slice all of the vegetables except the beets and place them into a bowl of ice water. Chill the vegetables for at least 30 minutes to crisp. Slice the beets in a separate bowl of water and change the water several times until it runs clear. Then add some ice to the beets to crisp them as well.

To serve: Pour the jalapeño vinaigrette into the bottom of eight shallow bowls. Cut the salmon into quarter-inch-thick slices and lay them in the center of each bowl. Toss the shaved salad in the vinaigrette and place it on top of the salmon.

**MIKE EMERSON,
PAPPY'S SMOKE-
HOUSE**

**What is your favorite
five-ingredient dish?**
Caprese salad.

**What's the name of
your favorite restaurant
(that's not your own)?**
My favorite restaurant is
Mai Sidney Haus Taria.
There, see if you can figure
that one out.

**Which kitchen tool do
you use the most?**
Aluminum foil. It's the
duct tape of our kitchen.

Pappy's Smokehouse Coleslaw

MIKE EMERSON, PAPPY'S SMOKEHOUSE

SERVES 6

- 1 large head cabbage, finely shredded
- 1 medium sweet onion, thinly sliced
- 2 carrots, peeled and grated
- 1 cup sugar
- 1 teaspoon salt
- $^2/_3$ cup vegetable oil
- 1 teaspoon dry mustard
- 1 teaspoon celery seed
- 1 cup cider vinegar

Combine the cabbage, onion, and grated carrots in a large serving bowl. In a saucepan over medium heat, combine the sugar, salt, vegetable oil, dry mustard, celery seed, and vinegar. Stir and heat the liquid until the sugar is dissolved. Pour the liquid over the vegetables and toss it well. Cover and refrigerate the slaw until it's thoroughly chilled.

SHREDDED CARROT SALAD WITH ORANGES, MINT, AND HARISSA

BEN POREMBA,
ELAIA, OLIO, AND SALUME BEDDU

SERVES 8

2 cups carrots, shredded

1 cup oranges, segmented

1/2 cup mint leaves, roughly chopped

1/2 cup Italian parsley, roughly chopped

2 lemons, juiced

1 teaspoon orange-blossom water

1/2 teaspoon ground cumin

1/2 teaspoon smoked paprika

1/2 teaspoon ground coriander

1 teaspoon garlic, minced

1 teaspoon chili paste (sambal oelek)

Salt

White pepper

1/4 cup extra-virgin olive oil

Toss together the shredded carrot, orange segments, mint, and parsley. To make the harissa dressing, whisk together the lemon juice, orange-blossom water, cumin, smoked paprika, coriander, garlic, chili paste, and salt and white pepper to taste. As you're whisking, drizzle in the olive oil. Pour the dressing over the salad and serve. This salad is usually served as a first course or a side dish for grilled fish, chicken, or lamb.

TUSCAN SHRIMP SALAD

KATIE LEE, KATIE'S PIZZERIA CAFÉ

SERVES 1

5 large shrimp, peeled and deveined

2 lemons, halved

Kosher salt

1/4 cup extra-virgin olive oil

1 large handful arugula

1 cup fennel bulb, thinly sliced

1/4 cup Kalamata olives

1 clementine, peeled and separated

1/4 cup pistachios, shelled

1/4 cup shaved Parmesan

Black pepper

Marinate the shrimp with the juice of one lemon and kosher salt to taste. Then pan-sear the shrimp in a hot pan with a little of the extra-virgin olive oil. When they're cooked through, set them aside.

To serve: Place the arugula, fennel bulb, olives, clementine wedges, and pistachios on a plate. Top the mix with the shrimp and shaved Parmesan. Squeeze the remaining lemon over the top and drizzle the salad with the remaining extra-virgin olive oil. Add salt and pepper to taste.

CASTRO-MUSSOLINI BRAISED PORK SANDWICH

MATHIS STITT, VERITAS GATEWAY TO FOOD AND WINE

SERVES 6

1 1/2 cups red wine

1 cup coffee

1/4 cup diced tomatoes with juice

1 tablespoon unsweetened cocoa powder

1 tablespoon salt

1/4 teaspoon cayenne pepper

1/4 cup dark chocolate, chopped

1 teaspoon Dijon mustard

2 pounds boneless pork shoulder

Salt

Vegetable oil

2 medium-size carrots, peeled

1 large onion

2 stalks celery

6 4-inch sections soft Italian-style baguette, sliced lengthwise

Mayonnaise

1 jar spicy pickle slices

1 pound prosciutto, thinly sliced

1 1/2 pound sliced Taleggio cheese (substitute mozzarella for a milder flavor)

To make the braising liquid, combine the red wine, coffee, tomatoes and their juice, cocoa powder, salt, cayenne pepper, chopped dark chocolate, and Dijon mustard in a large pot. Heat the mixture to a simmer, stirring periodically. Make sure all dry ingredients are incorporated and the chocolate is completely melted.

Cut the pork shoulder into six roughly equal pieces and season it with salt. Sear all sides of the meat in 1/4 inch of vegetable oil in a hot cast-iron skillet. Cook the meat until it's well-caramelized.

Preheat the oven to 275 degrees. Arrange the meat in a single layer in an appropriate-size oven-safe pot. Cut the carrots, onion, and celery into large pieces and add them to the pot with the meat. Pour the simmering braising liquid into the pot until it's three-quarters of the way up the side of the meat. Cover the pot with a lid or aluminum foil and place it in the oven.

Cook 4 to 6 hours until the meat is very tender; check the tenderness of the meat periodically with a fork.

Create each sandwich by spreading mayonnaise on the inside of each half of the baguette section. On the bottom half, place one piece of pork, and loosely pull it apart to cover the bread. Layer spicy pickles (as many or few as you like) on top of the pork, then place prosciutto on top of the pickles. Finish with the cheese, then cover the sandwich with the top half of the bread.

Toast the sandwich in a panini maker or a hot skillet, or bake it on a sheet pan in a 350-degree oven until the cheese is melted.

French Bean–and–Roquefort Salad

BRYAN CARR, POMME RESTAURANT, POMME CAFÉ, AND ATLAS RESTAURANT

SERVES 4

¼ cup red-wine vinegar

1 cup extra-virgin olive oil

1 handful fresh chives, chopped

Salt and fresh black pepper

Water

12 ounces fresh French green beans, a.k.a. *haricots verts*

4 ounces Roquefort cheese

1 handful almonds, toasted, sliced or slivered

1 tomato, peeled, seeded, and diced

Whisk together the vinegar and oil to make a vinaigrette. Add the chives and season with salt and pepper to taste.

Bring a large pot of water to a rolling boil. Prepare a bowl of ice water. Cook the green beans until they're tender but still slightly firm to the bite. They should not crunch when bitten. Strain the beans and plunge them into the ice water until they're thoroughly chilled. Do not let them soak in the water after they have cooled; remove them to a dish and let them dry.

Toss the beans in the vinaigrette with the Roquefort, almonds, and tomato. (For best results, do not substitute a lesser-quality blue cheese.) Arrange on four plates. Serve.

CLUB MED SANDWICH

MARK LUCAS,
FOZZIE'S SANDWICH EMPORIUM

SERVES 4

4 4-ounce chicken breasts

5 garlic cloves, peeled and minced

$1/2$ cup vegetable oil

1 medium sprig fresh rosemary, stemmed and chopped

4 sprigs fresh oregano, stemmed and chopped

8 sprigs fresh thyme, stemmed and chopped

2 red peppers, peeled, stemmed, and seeded, sliced into $1/4$-inch strips

Salt and pepper

2 lemons, juiced

$1/2$ cup olive oil

1 large zucchini, sliced into $1/8$-inch wheels

1 large yellow squash, sliced into $1/8$-inch wheels

4 wheat pitas

8 ounces goat cheese

8 ounces arugula

Marinate the chicken with two of the minced garlic cloves, $1/4$ cup of the vegetable oil, the chopped rosemary and oregano, and half of the chopped thyme. Mix the ingredients well and place the chicken in the refrigerator.

Preheat the oven to 425 degrees. Put the red-pepper strips in a bowl and mix them with the remaining $1/4$ cup vegetable oil and a pinch of salt and pepper. Spread the strips on a sheet tray, then bake the peppers for 20 minutes, turning them over halfway through. Remove the roasted peppers from the oven, place them in a bowl, and cover it with plastic wrap. Lower the oven to 350.

To make the lemon-thyme vinaigrette, combine the lemon juice with the remaining thyme and minced garlic, then whisk in the olive oil. Season the mixture with salt and pepper to taste and set it aside. Take the chicken out and cut it into $1/2$–inch strips.

Cook the chicken and marinade in a sauté pan over high heat, stirring occasionally, until the chicken is browned. Then add the zucchini, squash, roasted peppers, and salt and pepper to taste. Sauté the chicken and vegetables for 3 to 5 minutes, or until the zucchini and squash are tender.

Place the pitas on a sheet tray. Spread chunks of goat cheese on top of each and warm them in the oven for 8 minutes.

Evenly portion the chicken and vegetables on half of each pita. Toss the arugula in a bowl with the lemon-thyme vinaigrette and place it on other half of the pita. Serve the sandwich immediately, so it's warm.

EL JIBARITO

BOB BRAZELL, GRINGO, AND
STEVE CARAVELLI, FORMERLY GRINGO

SERVES 4

Pork belly *al pastor* (see recipe)

8 tostones (see recipe)

Tomato-chipotle jam (see recipe)

Pickled red onion (see recipe)

Fresh arugula

Fresh cilantro

PORK BELLY *AL PASTOR*

1 pound fresh pork belly, skin removed

$1/4$ cup onion, chopped

1 cup pineapple, diced

2 tablespoons orange juice

1 tablespoon distilled white vinegar

1 tablespoon Guajillo powder (chili powder
   may be substituted)

1 garlic clove, peeled

½ teaspoon ground cumin

½ teaspoon achiote paste

1 chipotle chili in adobo sauce, plus
   1 teaspoon of sauce from the can

1 teaspoon kosher salt

To make the marinade, combine all the ingredients besides the pork belly in a blender and purée them until they're smooth. Pour this over the pork belly and let it marinate for 6 to 12 hours in the refrigerator. Then cook the pork belly in a covered pot or pan in a 300-degree oven for 3 to 4 hours, or until tender. Remove the pork belly from the oven, place the meat between two sheets of parchment paper, then place it between two sheet pans or large plates. Put weights on top and put the meat in the refrigerator until it's completely chilled. Flattening the pork belly makes the meat easier to slice.

TOSTONES

4 plantains

Vegetable oil

Salt

With a small sharp knife, cut the ends off of each plantain and cut a lengthwise slit through the skin along its inside curve. Beginning in the center of the slit, pry the skin off of the plantain and cut the plantain in half crosswise.

In a deep fryer or large skillet, heat 4 inches of oil to 360 degrees. Fry the eight plantain pieces two at a time for 1 ½ to 2 minutes, or until they are a pale golden. With a slotted spoon, transfer the pieces to paper towels to drain briefly.

Working quickly, using a tortilla press or the flat bottom of a bottle, flatten each piece between sheets of wax paper to a thickness of no less than ¼ to ⅓ inch. Refry the flattened, cooled pieces in the 360-degree oil, turning them occasionally for 2 to 3 minutes, or until they're golden.

Use the slotted spoon to transfer the tostones to paper towels to drain, and season them with salt. The tostones should be crisp on the outside and chewy on the inside.

TOMATO-CHIPOTLE JAM

2 teaspoons vegetable oil

¼ cup onion, diced

1 teaspoon minced garlic

1 28-ounce can crushed tomatoes

1 chipotle chili in adobo sauce

¼ cup honey

2 teaspoons sugar

Kosher salt

Heat the vegetable oil and sauté the onion and garlic until they're soft. Add the tomatoes, chipotle chili, honey, sugar, and kosher salt to taste and cook the jam for about 30 to 45 minutes at a low simmer. Stir frequently to avoid burning. Allow the jam to cool slightly and transfer it to the base of a food processor or blender; process it until it's smooth. Strain the jam through a fine mesh sieve and refrigerate it.

PICKLED RED ONION

2 cups cider vinegar

1 cup water

1 teaspoon dried oregano, preferably Mexican

½ cup sugar

1 tablespoon salt

1 red onion, julienned

Place the cider vinegar, water, oregano, sugar, and salt in a saucepan and bring it to a boil. Place the julienned onions in a nonreactive container and pour in the hot pickling liquid. Cover the container with plastic wrap and allow it to cool to room temperature.

To serve this local twist on a Puerto Rican–American fried plantain sandwich: Cut the pork belly into 1/4–inch slices and crisp the slices in a hot skillet. Spread 1 to 2 teaspoons of tomato-chipotle jam on each tostone. Set four tostones, jam side up, on a plate. Place three or four slices of pork on each of the tostones. Top the pork with pickled red onion, arugula, and cilantro. Place one of the four remaining tostones, jam side down, on top to complete each sandwich. Serve the sandwiches with the remaining jam on the side for dipping.

THE WORLD'S BEST MEATLOAF MELT

ISABEL BIESTERFELD, JENNIFER'S PHARMACY & SODA SHOPPE

MAKES 10 SANDWICHES

FOR EACH SANDWICH

- 2 slices white bread
- 2 slices American cheese
- 2 thin slices meatloaf (see recipe)
- 1 tablespoon ketchup
- Pickles (optional)
- Chips

MEATLOAF

- 2 eggs
- 1 1/2 pound ground chuck
- 2 tablespoons onion, chopped
- 3/4 cup dried bread crumbs

- Worcestershire sauce
- Milk
- Dried oregano
- 1 1/2 cups of your favorite barbecue sauce
- 1 teaspoon salt
- 1/2 teaspoon pepper

Preheat the oven to 350 degrees. Whisk the eggs and add the ground beef, onion, bread crumbs, a dash of Worcestershire sauce, a dash of milk, a dash of oregano, 3/4 cup of the barbecue sauce, salt, and pepper. Knead the mixture together and mold it into a loaf pan.

Bake the meatloaf for 60 minutes, or until an internal thermometer reaches 160 degrees. Remove it from the oven and drain the grease. Pour the remaining barbecue sauce on top and return the meatloaf to the oven for 15 minutes. Let the meatloaf cool and slice it.

For each sandwich, take two pieces of bread (preferably white) and place one piece of American cheese on each side. Put two thin slices of meatloaf on the bread along with the ketchup. Close up the sandwich and grill it on a panini machine until the cheese melts and the bread is brown. Slice the sandwich diagonally and serve it with pickles (optional) and chips.

PORTOBELLO BURGER WITH SHERRY ZUCCHINI AND YELLOW SQUASH RIBBONS

JENNIFER PENSONEAU,
J.FIRES' MARKET BISTRO

SERVES 1

1 portobello mushroom

2 sprigs each of parsley, thyme, basil, and oregano

½ cup extra-virgin olive oil

Sherry zucchini and yellow squash ribbons (see recipe)

Rosemary-sherry mayonnaise (see recipe)

1 hamburger bun

Clean the portobello mushroom by wiping it off and cutting off the gill part underneath the cap. Preheat the oven to 450 degrees. Place the mushroom in an ovenproof pan. Place the herbs on the mushroom, pour the oil on top, and roast it for 25 minutes.

ROSEMARY-SHERRY MAYONNAISE

1 1-inch sprig of rosemary, leaves finely minced

1 tablespoon sherry

½ cup mayonnaise

In a mixing bowl, combine the rosemary, sherry, and mayonnaise.

SHERRY ZUCCHINI AND YELLOW SQUASH RIBBONS

¼ cup raw sugar

½ cup water

¼ cup sherry

2 zucchini

2 yellow squash

Mix the sugar and water together over heat to form a syrup, then add the sherry. Take the liquid off the heat and let it cool. Wash the vegetables. Peel the vegetables lengthwise into thinly sliced ribbons. Once the sherry mix is cool, pour it over the ribbons and let them marinate in a covered container for at least 4 hours.

To serve: Toast the hamburger bun. Warm the sherry zucchini and yellow squash ribbons in a sauté pan over medium heat. Layer the bun with the portobello and the ribbons, then spread rosemary-sherry mayonnaise on top.

CHICKEN-AND-MUSHROOM SOUP

FRAZER CAMERON, FRAZER'S RESTAURANT & LOUNGE

SERVES 8

½ cup fresh garlic cloves, peeled

Water

1 ½ cups chicken stock

6 tablespoons unsalted butter

6 tablespoons yellow onion, diced

½ pound mushrooms, sliced

⅓ cup flour

1 whole fryer chicken, roasted

1 ½ cups milk

¾ cup cream

1 small bunch parsley, chopped

Boil the fresh peeled garlic cloves in a simmering pot of water for 12 minutes. Drain the garlic and boil it

CONTINUED ON PG. 50

**BEN POREMBA,
ELAIA, OLIO, AND
SALUME BEDDU**

**What is your favorite
comfort food?** Fried
chicken.

**Your favorite restaurant
(aside from your own)?**
Sameem Afghan Restaurant.

One great cooking tip?
Use more salt, finish with
good-quality extra-virgin
olive oil, use medium heat.

**Which kitchen tool do
you use the most?**
My 8-inch chef's knife.

Chilled Pea Soup with Yogurt, Trout Roe, and Mint

BEN POREMBA, ELAIA, OLIO, AND SALUME BEDDU

SERVES 6

¼ cup extra-virgin olive oil

1 cup celery root, diced

1 cup leeks, white part only, diced

1 cup dry vermouth, preferably
  Noilly Prat

1 pound frozen sweet peas

Mineral water

Salt

White pepper

Cayenne pepper

Lime juice

Crème fraîche, optional

Plain Greek yogurt

Mint leaves

Lime zest

Chives, chopped

Trout roe

Heat the olive oil in a heavy pot. Add the celery root and leek and slowly sweat the vegetables on medium-low heat until they're softened, 10 to 12 minutes. Don't let the vegetables brown. Raise the heat and deglaze the pot with the vermouth. Add the frozen peas and enough mineral water to just cover them. Bring the pot to a boil, then remove it from the stove. Purée the soup in a blender until it's very smooth. If the soup is too thick, add more mineral water. Season it with plenty of salt, white pepper, cayenne pepper, and lime juice, then let it chill for at least 2 hours. You may add a touch of crème fraîche.

Pour the soup and garnish the plate with high-quality plain Greek yogurt, torn mint leaves, lime zest, chopped chives, and trout roe.

Clam Chowder

JODI ALLEN GORDON, COMPANION

SERVES 10

½ cup yellow onion, diced

1 cup carrots, diced

1 cup celery, diced

1 bay leaf

2 tablespoons butter

1 head garlic, peeled

Olive oil

Salt and pepper

32 ounces clams with juice, chopped

3 cups vegetable stock

2 cups potatoes, peeled and diced

1 cup heavy cream

4 tablespoons butter

4 tablespoons flour

Sauté the onion, carrots, and celery with the bay leaf in 2 tablespoons of butter until the vegetables are softened, about 10 minutes.

Preheat the oven to 350 degrees. Place the peeled head of garlic in a ramekin, pour enough olive oil over it to cover it, and season it with salt and pepper. Roast it in the oven until it's brown and caramelized, about 20 minutes. Let the garlic cool, then purée it.

Add the puréed garlic to the vegetables. Add the chopped clams and their juice. Add the vegetable stock and bring the liquid to a boil. Add the potatoes and cook the soup until they're soft, about 20 minutes. Add the heavy cream and return the soup to a boil. In a separate pot, melt 4 tablespoons of butter, whisk in the flour, and cook it a couple of minutes to form a light roux. Whisk the roux thoroughly into the boiling soup.

Taste the soup and season it with salt and pepper to taste, if necessary. Remove the bay leaf before serving.

again in fresh water for 10 more minutes. Strain out the garlic and discard the water. In a food processor or blender, purée the cooked garlic with the chicken stock until it's smooth.

In a 4-quart pot, sauté the diced onion with the butter until it's tender. Add the sliced mushrooms and cook it for 5 minutes more. Sprinkle in the flour and cook, stirring continuously for 2 minutes. Take care not to burn the flour. After 2 minutes, slowly add the purée of garlic and chicken stock. Keep stirring until the purée is incorporated into the rest of the ingredients. There should be no lumps. Bring the soup to a simmer and cook it for 30 minutes.

Cut the meat off of the roasted chicken and cut it into small pieces. Add it to the soup and bring the liquid back to a simmer.

Bring the milk and cream to a simmer and add it to the hot soup. If the soup is too thick at this point, add extra chicken stock. If it's too thin, continue to reduce the liquid at a very low simmer, stirring often. After ladling the soup into bowls, garnish it with the chopped parsley.

CORN SOUP WITH CHERRY TOMATO– AND–BASIL SALAD

JOSHUA ROLAND, CONSULTING CHEF

SERVES 6

CORN SOUP

- 1 cup fresh corn kernels
- 3 cups chicken stock
- 1 shallot, sliced
- Salt and pepper
- Cherry tomato–and–basil salad (see recipe)

Place the corn, chicken stock, and shallot in a pot and bring it to a simmer. Season it with salt and pepper to taste. Simmer the soup on low heat until the corn is tender, about 5 minutes. Place the soup in a blender and purée it until it's smooth and naturally creamy.

CHERRY TOMATO–AND–BASIL SALAD

- 1 tablespoon extra-virgin olive oil
- 1 teaspoon red-wine vinegar
- 1 small shallot, sliced thin
- 1 tablespoon assorted basil, torn
- Salt and pepper
- 1 cup assorted cherry tomatoes, halved

Whisk the olive oil, red-wine vinegar, shallot, and basil with salt and pepper to taste. Pour this dressing over the tomatoes and let them marinate for at least 30 minutes at room temperature before garnishing the soup. Serve the soup hot or cold, garnished with the cherry tomato– and–basil salad.

GAZPACHO WITH AVOCADO AND CRAB

BRYAN CARR,

POMME RESTAURANT, POMME CAFÉ & WINE BAR, AND ATLAS RESTAURANT

SERVES 4 WITH LEFTOVERS

GAZPACHO

- 2 pounds fresh, ripe tomatoes
- 1 14-ounce can Roma tomatoes
- 1 onion, quartered
- 4 cloves fresh garlic, peeled
- 2 stalks celery
- 1 cucumber, peeled and seeded
- 1 bunch parsley, stems removed

6 sprigs fresh tarragon, stems removed

1 tablespoon fennel seeds

6 ounces stale white bread, preferably French

1 green bell pepper, seeded

1 red bell pepper, seeded

¼ cup olive oil

In a blender or food processor, combine the tomatoes, onion, garlic, celery, cucumber, parsley, tarragon, fennel, stale bread, and peppers. Purée the mixture until it's smooth. With the machine running, pour in the olive oil. Strain the purée into a large container. Chill it for at least 3 hours. The soup should be very cold.

AVOCADO-CRAB SALAD

1 ripe avocado

8 ounces lump crabmeat, picked over for any shell particles

2 tablespoons olive oil

3 dashes fresh lemon juice

Salt and fresh black pepper

Peel and dice the avocado. Fold the avocado and crab together and season the mixture with the olive oil and lemon juice, plus salt and pepper to taste. Chill.

To serve: Set out four broad soup plates. In the center of each plate, place a mound of avocado-crab salad. Pour the gazpacho around the crab.

LEMONGRASS-CUCUMBER GAZPACHO

CALLAGHAN CARTER, BIXBY'S

SERVES 8

1 stalk lemongrass, broken and chopped

1 small whole fresh cayenne pepper

4 whole ripe summer tomatoes

2 teaspoons garlic, minced

2 tablespoons tomato paste

¼ cup dry white wine

16 ounces tomato juice

1 tablespoon ginger root, finely grated

1 bunch scallions, sliced

¼ cup olive oil

2 limes, zested and juiced

2 dashes fish sauce

1 English cucumber, peeled, seeded, and roughly chopped

½ bunch cilantro with stems, roughly chopped

Salt

In a heavy-bottomed pan on medium-high heat, cook the lemongrass, the cayenne pepper, the tomatoes, and 1 teaspoon of the minced garlic for 10 minutes. Then add the tomato paste. Stir to almost roast the paste. Add the white wine and reduce the liquid to cook off the alcohol. Add half of the tomato juice. Purée the mixture in a blender until it's smooth and strain it through a fine sieve. Set it aside.

In the same pan, add the grated ginger, scallions, 1 teaspoon of the minced garlic, and olive oil. Cook this on medium heat for about 10 minutes. Add the reserved purée and the rest of the tomato juice. Turn off the heat and allow the mixture to cool. Add the lime juice, lime zest, fish sauce, cucumber, cilantro, and salt to taste.

Purée the soup, either roughly or until it's smooth; it's great either way. Chill it, then serve.

Khao Soi Northern Thai Noodle Soup

PHATCHARIN WANNA, FORK & STIX

SERVES 4

2 tablespoons vegetable oil

3 to 4 tablespoons red curry paste

1/2 teaspoon turmeric powder

1 teaspoon yellow curry powder

4 cups coconut milk

2 to 3 pounds chicken or beef, cut into medium pieces (chicken legs and thighs may be used)

1 1/2 cups water or chicken stock

1/2 tablespoon sugar

Fish sauce (optional)

4 cups vegetable oil

1 package Chinese egg noodles

Water

1/2 cup shallots, peeled and thinly sliced

1/2 cup Thai pickled mustard greens, thinly sliced

1/2 cup cilantro, chopped

3 tablespoons dried chilies

1 lime, cut into wedges

Note: The Chinese egg noodles and Thai pickled mustard greens, as well as all other ingredients, can be purchased at Jay International Foods (3172 S. Grand, 314-772-2552).

To make the curry broth, heat the vegetable oil in a pot over medium heat. Then add the red curry paste, turmeric, and yellow curry powder. Stir for a few minutes, until the curry paste is fragrant. Stir in about 2 cups of the coconut milk. Turn the heat to high and bring the sauce to a boil. Stir the pot and wait for the red oil to separate from the coconut milk. Add the chicken or beef, 1 1/2 cups of water or chicken stock, and remaining coconut milk. Bring the sauce back to boil, then turn down the heat to simmer until the meat is done. Stir in the sugar, and optionally add fish sauce to taste for a salty element.

To fry the noodles, first heat 4 cups vegetable oil to 350 degrees in a medium-size pot. Separate the Chinese egg noodles into individual strands and fry them, a small portion at a time, until they're golden brown. Drain the noodles and place them on a dry paper towel to rest and cool.

Bring a pot of water to a boil, then add the egg noodles and cook them for 5 to 8 minutes. Once the noodles are cooked, rinse them in cold water to remove excess starch, then drain the excess water. (An extra 1/2 tablespoon of oil can be added to prevent the noodles from sticking together.)

For the garnish, place the thinly sliced shallots, Thai pickled mustard greens, chopped cilantro, and dried chilies in separate bowls.

To serve: Place the cooked noodles in a bowl, top it with the hot curry broth and crispy noodles, and add the shallots, Thai pickled mustard greens, and cilantro. Spoon the dried chilies on the side. Squeeze a wedge of lime over the dish before eating.

PORTUGUESE TOMATO SOUP

CHRIS LEE, RIVER CITY CASINO

SERVES 8

¼ cup olive oil

1 cup yellow onion, diced

¼ cup garlic, peeled and minced

2 bay leaves

1 teaspoon hot smoked paprika

1 tablespoon cumin seeds, toasted and
   crushed in a mortar

1 tablespoon coriander seeds, toasted and
   crushed in a mortar

4 pounds ripe tomatoes or 2 large cans
   whole peeled tomatoes

1 cup dry white wine

1 ½ cups chicken stock

Salt and pepper

Sherry vinegar

2 cups baguette, torn into chunks, tossed in
   olive oil, and lightly toasted

½ cup Manchego or Asiago cheese, shaved

8 eggs, poached

1 ½ cups cilantro leaves, torn

Extra-virgin olive oil

Cilantro

In a stockpot, heat the olive oil over medium-high
heat. Add the onion and cook until it's soft and lightly
colored. Add the minced garlic, bay leaves, paprika,
cumin, and coriander and cook the mix until it's
fragrant. Add ²/₃ of the tomatoes and cook them for
5 minutes. Then add the wine and stock, bring it to a
simmer, and cook it for 10 minutes. Remove the bay
leaves and pass the soup through a food mill.

Return the soup to the pot and season it to taste
with salt and pepper. If the soup is too thick, add more
stock. Taste the soup and adjust its acidity with a touch
of sherry vinegar. Divide the remaining tomatoes, the
bread chunks, and the cheese among eight bowls. Place
a poached egg in the center of each bowl and ladle the
hot soup over it. Garnish each bowl with extra-virgin
olive oil and cilantro.

ROASTED RED PEPPER BISQUE

JODI ALLEN GORDON, COMPANION

SERVES 12

1 28-ounce can roasted red peppers

4 garlic cloves, minced

1 cup yellow onion, diced

2 tablespoons olive oil

3 cups chicken stock

2 cups dry white wine

2 cups fresh basil, chopped

Salt and pepper

2 cups evaporated milk

2 cups half-and-half

Drain and chop the roasted red peppers, and discard
the liquid. Purée the peppers and set them aside. Sauté
the garlic and onion in olive oil until it's tender. Add the
chicken stock. Reduce the liquid by half. Add the white
wine and reduce the liquid again by half. Add the basil
and puréed peppers, plus salt and pepper to taste. Heat
the liquid again for 5 minutes over low heat. Remove it
from the heat and blend it in a food processor until it's
smooth. Return it to low heat and add the evaporated
milk and half-and-half. Simmer the soup for another
5 minutes before serving.

SPRING ASPARAGUS SOUP WITH PARMIGIANO-REGGIANO ZABAGLIONE

BOB COLOSIMO,
ELEVEN ELEVEN MISSISSIPPI

SERVES 4 TO 6

2 tablespoons butter

1 small onion, diced small

1 stalk celery, diced small

3 cups vegetable or chicken broth

8 cups asparagus, separated into stalks and tips

1/2 cup cornstarch

1/2 cup cold water

1/2 cup cream

Salt and pepper

Hot pepper sauce (optional)

Parmigiano-Reggiano zabaglione (see recipe)

In a medium-size saucepot, sauté the onion and celery in the butter for 5 minutes. Add the broth and asparagus stalks. Simmer this for 30 minutes, or until the asparagus is very tender. Then remove the pot from the heat and purée the contents with a hand-held immersion blender. Strain the purée through a fine strainer, if desired.

Mix the cornstarch and water. Return the purée to the heat and bring it to a simmer. Slowly whisk the cornstarch mixture into the simmering soup. Add the cream and season the soup with salt, pepper, and optionally hot sauce to taste. Add the asparagus tips and simmer the soup for 5 minutes. Adjust the seasoning to taste.

PARMIGIANO-REGGIANO ZABAGLIONE

Water

2 large egg yolks

2 tablespoons dry white wine

Kosher salt

1/2 cup Parmigiano-Reggiano cheese, grated

1/4 cup whipping cream, whipped into soft peaks

Fresh ground black pepper

Hot pepper sauce (optional)

Pour 1 inch of water into a medium saucepan and bring it to a simmer. In a medium-size bowl, add the egg yolks, wine, and a pinch of kosher salt. Place the bowl over the simmering water and whisk constantly until the mixture is very thick. Don't let the mixture get too hot, or the eggs will scramble.

Whisking constantly, add the grated cheese and continue to whisk the mixture for 1 more minute. Remove it from the heat and let it cool to room temperature. Fold in the whipped cream, being careful to keep the mixture light and fluffy. Season the zabaglione with salt, black pepper, and optionally hot sauce to taste.

JODI ALLEN GORDON, COMPANION

Who taught you to cook?
My parents. My whole family loves to cook.

Your favorite cookbook?
Anything by Ina Garten.

Which kitchen tool do you use most? Offset spatula.

What ingredient must every pantry have? Black pepper—my favorite spice.

What is your favorite five-ingredient dish? Soup.

Spicy Vegetarian Chili

JODI ALLEN GORDON, COMPANION

SERVES 24

3 pounds eggplant, cubed

3 tablespoons olive oil, plus extra to coat the eggplant

6 onions, diced

9 garlic cloves, diced

1 can roasted red peppers, diced

5 jalapeño peppers, seeded and diced

6 zucchini, diced

1 No. 10 can diced tomatoes

2 tablespoons oregano

3 tablespoons ground cumin

3 tablespoons chili powder

1 tablespoon fennel seed

1 No. 10 can white beans, drained and rinsed

1 No. 10 can kidney beans, drained and rinsed

4 lemons, zested

9 tablespoons lemon juice

1 tablespoon sugar

1 cup cilantro, chopped

Kosher salt

Black pepper

Cheddar cheese, grated

Sour cream

Preheat the oven to 450 degrees. Place the diced eggplant in a bowl and lightly toss it with enough olive oil to coat it. Place it in a roasting pan, cover it with foil, and bake it for 30 minutes.

In a large stockpot, heat 3 tablespoons of olive oil. Add the onions and cook them until they're translucent. Add the garlic and cook it until it's fragrant, about another minute. Add the peppers, zucchini, and jalapeños. Cook the vegetables for about 5 minutes, stirring often. Add the diced tomatoes and all the liquid in the can. Add the oregano, cumin, chili powder, and fennel seed.

Carefully stir in the eggplant and simmer the chili for 20 minutes over very low heat. Add the white beans, kidney beans, lemon zest, lemon juice, sugar, and cilantro. Add salt and pepper to taste. Simmer the chili for 10 minutes. Top each bowl with shredded cheddar and sour cream before serving it.

SUMMER SQUASH "CARPACCIO"

PATRICK CONNOLLY, BASSO

SERVES 4

RICOTTA

- 1 quart whole milk
- 1 cup heavy cream
- 6 lemons, juiced
- 1 orange, zested
- 1 sprig rosemary
- Salt

In a heavy-bottomed stockpot, combine the milk, cream, lemon juice, orange zest, and rosemary. Heat this mixture to 175 degrees, then remove it from the heat and let it rest for 15 minutes.

Strain the pot's contents into a colander lined with cheesecloth and over a bowl. Cover the bowl and let the cheese drip for several hours or up to one day, depending on how wet or dry you prefer the ricotta to be. Once done, season it to taste with salt. Transfer the remaining curds to a bowl, cover, and refrigerate.

CARPACCIO

- 1 cup vegetable oil
- 1/4 cup capers
- 2 pounds mixed summer squash
- 2 lemons, halved
- 4 tablespoons extra-virgin olive oil
- 1 tablespoon sea salt
- Pepper
- 4 sprigs basil

In a large pot, heat the vegetable oil to 350 degrees. Drain and dry the capers, then fry them in the vegetable oil until they're crispy, about 1 minute.

Remove the capers from the oil and let them drain on a paper towel.

Shave the squash into very thin slices with a mandoline. Shingle the squash to cover the surface of four plates. Squeeze half a lemon and drizzle olive oil onto each plate. Season with the sea salt and pepper. Sprinkle the fried capers and basil leaves on top. Take 4 ounces of the fresh ricotta and spoon it around the plates. Serve the dish cold or at room temperature.

THE MUSHROOM SOUP

ISSAC HARDWRICT, ECLIPSE

SERVES 4

- 1 1/4 pound thick-cut bacon, diced
- 1 pound wild mushrooms, cleaned and coarsely chopped
- Salt and pepper
- Onion
- Celery
- 1/2 cup parsley, chopped
- 1/2 tablespoon ground coriander
- 1/4 tablespoon ground thyme
- 1 tablespoon soy sauce
- 1 1/4 quart half-and-half
- 1 to 2 tablespoons all-purpose flour
- 1 ounce smoked Gouda cheese

In a heavy-bottomed pan, dice and render the bacon. Remove the bacon from the fat. Reserve the fat in the pan.

Preheat the oven to 350 degrees. Season the mushrooms with salt and pepper to taste and roast them in the oven for 10 to 12 minutes.

In the pan, sauté the onion, celery, and roasted mushrooms in half of the bacon fat until the onion is caramelized. Add in the spices, soy sauce, and half-and-half and bring the liquid to a slow simmer.

As it simmers, begin making the roux. Heat the remaining half of the bacon fat. Working on a 1-to-1 ratio, mix the fat and flour. Stir constantly, until the roux is golden brown or darker. Low and slow is the key.

Add 1 to 2 tablespoons of the roux to the simmering soup to thicken it.

To serve: Pour the soup into oven-proof bowls. Top each with $1/4$ ounce of the smoked Gouda cheese and broil the soup until the cheese is melted and bubbly.

Appetizers

ASIAN BARBECUE SPARE RIBS

NY VONGSALY, BAR LES FRÈRES, BOBO NOODLE HOUSE, AND I FRATELLINI

SERVES 6 TO 8

½ cup sesame oil

1 cup honey

1 cup soy sauce

½ cup Asian chili paste

1 teaspoon garlic, chopped

1 teaspoon fresh ginger, chopped in a food processor

4 to 6 pounds spare ribs, in racks

Salt and pepper

Preheat the oven to 325 degrees or preheat a grill to medium low. To make the sauce, whisk together the sesame oil, honey, soy sauce, chili paste, garlic, and ginger. Season the spare ribs with salt and pepper, and place them on a cookie sheet in the oven or directly on the grill. Cook the ribs for 45 to 50 minutes, turning them frequently until they're golden brown. Baste them with the sauce and cook them for 10 to 15 minutes more. Slice the racks of ribs into individual ribs and brush them with more of the remaining sauce. These ribs are delicious hot, room-temperature, or cold the next day.

BAKED OLIVES

DANA HOLLAND, JILLY'S CUPCAKE BAR & CAFÉ

SERVES 12 TO 15

This dish is great for entertaining, served with crusty bread

or as part of an antipasto platter. The olives become lush and velvety, and the oil develops a fantastic flavor.

2 pounds assorted olives (large green and black Bella di Cerignola olives are recommended), with pits

3 cups olive oil

1 orange, zested

2 sprigs fresh rosemary

1 teaspoon red-pepper flakes

24 garlic cloves (2 to 3 heads of garlic), unpeeled

2 loaves ciabatta or focaccia bread

Parmigiano-Reggiano, chipped into nuggets

Preheat the oven to 250 degrees. Rinse the olives and dry them very well. Place them in a heatproof dish, no deeper than 3 inches. Add enough olive oil to cover the olives. Add the orange zest, rosemary, red-pepper flakes, and garlic. Cover the dish with a lid or foil and place it in the oven. Bake the olives for 45 minutes, then check whether they're tender and the garlic is soft. If not, continue baking for another 15 minutes.

When the olives are tender, remove the dish from the oven, uncover it, and allow it to cool for at least 5 minutes before serving. If you're making the olives ahead of time, store them in a sealed container and reheat them in an ovenproof vessel in a 300-degree oven until they're warm to the touch, about 10 minutes.

Serve the olives and garlic with ciabatta or focaccia bread. Squeeze the garlic onto the bread. When the olive oil has cooled, add some nuggets of Parmigiano-Reggiano to it to macerate.

Note: The oil is also delicious as a dip for raw veggies, like sliced fennel bulb, sweet peppers, celery, and endive; strained, it's perfect on pasta, for making bruschetta, or for salad dressings.

BISTRO MUSSELS
JON LOWE, OCEANO BISTRO
SERVES 4

2 tablespoons vegetable oil

24 Prince Edward Island mussels, cleaned

1 tablespoon shallots, sliced

1 Roma tomato, chopped

5 cloves garlic, roasted (see recipe)

1/4 cup white wine

3/4 cup shellfish stock (see recipe)

2 tablespoons butter, cold

1 tablespoon fresh basil, chopped

Salt and pepper

In a sauté pan, heat the vegetable oil on high. Add the mussels and cook for 1 minute. Then add the shallots, tomato, and roasted garlic. Deglaze the pan with the white wine. Add the shellfish stock and cover the pan. Simmer it on high heat until the mussels start to open. Remove the cover. Add the butter and basil. Season with salt and pepper to taste.

Note: A nice baguette or rustic-style bread goes well with this dish; it's great for soaking up that wonderful sauce in the bottom of the bowl.

ROASTED GARLIC

1 head (5 cloves) garlic, unpeeled

Vegetable oil

Preheat the oven to 350 degrees. Cut off the top of the head of garlic and lightly drizzle it with vegetable oil. Wrap it in foil and bake it for 20 minutes or until tender.

SHELLFISH STOCK

MAKES 3 QUARTS

2 tablespoons vegetable oil

1 whole lobster body's shells, meat removed and saved for another use

1/4 pound shrimp shells

1 cup tomato paste

1/2 cup white wine

1 carrot, unpeeled, roughly chopped

2 stalks celery, roughly chopped

1 jumbo yellow onion, unpeeled, roughly chopped

1 bulb fennel, roughly chopped

1 teaspoon crushed red chili flakes

1 bay leaf

4 sprigs fresh thyme

1 gallon water

In a large pot, heat the oil. Add the lobster body and shrimp shells. Fry the shells until they turn a bright pink. Stir in the tomato paste and coat the shells. Deglaze the pot with the white wine. Add the remaining ingredients and bring the stock to a boil, then reduce the heat to low. Let it simmer for 1 hour. Strain the stock through a fine mesh strainer.

Bacon Jelly
With Flatbread

MATHEW UNGER, MATHEW'S KITCHEN

MAKES 24 SERVINGS

BACON JAM

5 pounds applewood–
  smoked bacon, diced

2 pounds white onions,
  diced

1 ½ cups red wine
  vinegar

1 cup sugar

Salt and pepper

FLATBREAD

1 cup all purpose flour

½ cup semolina flour

1 ½ teaspoons baking
  powder

½ teaspoon salt

½ cup water

2 tablespoons olive oil

2 tablespoons blue
  cheese, crumbled

Cook the bacon in a large frying pan on low heat for 2 to 3 hours. Render the bacon slowly, so that the bits on the bottom don't burn. Much of the flavor from this dish comes from the goodness on the bottom of the pan. Remove half of the bacon fat from the pan. (Save it for another use, as there are many uses for leftover bacon fat.) Add the onions and cook them with the bacon until they are translucent, about 30 minutes. Deglaze the pan with red-wine vinegar.

Add the sugar to balance the dish's acidity, plus salt and pepper to taste. Let the jelly cook for another hour, or until the acid in the red-wine vinegar breaks down the bacon. Store the jelly in the refrigerator.

To make the flatbread: Make a well out of the dry ingredients (the flours, baking powder, and salt) and add the water and olive oil.

Let sit for 15 minutes. Roll the dough into a 12-inch round. Bake it at 375 degrees for 5 minutes before adding the bacon jelly and blue cheese. Bake an additional 5 to 8 minutes.

CARAMEL BRIE

DANA HOLLAND,
JILLY'S CUPCAKE BAR & CAFÉ

SERVES 6 TO 10

The chef and his wife love this dish, and it's perfect for entertaining. It's easy, fun, and can be made ahead of time. Though it's delicious unstuffed, Holland believes the macerated apricots or other dried fruits give it a wonderful boost in flavor. If you don't want to stuff the brie, skip to the caramel-making steps.

- 1/2 cup dried apricots (or craisins, dried cherries, or dried figs), diced
- 1/2 cup orange juice
- 1 tablespoon rum (optional)
- 1 15-ounce wheel brie
- 20 pecan halves
- 1/2 cup sugar
- 1/2 cup water
- 1/4 teaspoon ground black pepper, preferably fresh
- Bread, crackers, crostini, or lavash

To get started, put the dried fruit in a bowl. Warm the orange juice in a saucepan and pour it over the fruit. Add the rum, if you're using it. Stir the mixture, cover it, and set it aside.

To split the refrigerated wheel of brie, remove the wrapping and place the wheel on a flat surface. Cutting into the side of the cheese, place your knife horizontally in the middle of a side and slice a 2-inch-deep arc into the wheel. Turn the wheel 90 degrees and cut in again as before. Repeat this twice more, then cut all the way through. Remove the resulting "lid" and set it aside.

After the fruit has soaked for at least 30 minutes (this can be done 2 days ahead of time), spread it on the bottom half of the wheel of cheese. Replace the top of the brie and place it on the serving platter you will be using.

Toast the pecan halves in a 300-degree oven until they're golden, 7 to 10 minutes. Set them aside.

To make the caramel, put the sugar and water in a small saucepan and stir to dissolve the sugar. Bring the mixture to a boil to ensure the sugar is dissolved.

Lower the heat and simmer the syrup without stirring until it turns an amber color. Swirl in the black pepper. Remove the caramel syrup from the heat and let it cool for 1 minute. Pour it evenly over the brie. Immediately set the toasted pecan halves decoratively on top. Allow everything to cool, but do not refrigerate the brie at this point.

Crack the caramel shell with a spoon, then serve the brie with bread, crackers, crostini, or lavash.

CELERY ROOT–AND–FENNEL BRANDADE

BILL CARDWELL, CARDWELL'S AT THE
PLAZA AND BC'S KITCHEN

SERVES 6

- 1 1/2 pounds celery root, peeled and cut into medium dice
- 2 fennel bulbs, trimmed, cored, and quartered
- 2 large yellow potatoes, peeled and quartered
- 1 lemon, juiced
- Water
- 1/2 cup extra-virgin olive oil
- 4 cloves garlic, peeled (can add more to taste)
- 2/3 cup heavy cream
- 2 star anise pods
- Salt and freshly ground white pepper

2 tablespoons chopped parsley

1 loaf French bread, sliced and toasted

Drizzle the celery root, fennel, and potatoes with the lemon juice. Cook the vegetables in a steamer over simmering water until they're tender, about 20 minutes. Drain and keep them warm.

Heat the olive oil in a pan, add the garlic and cook until softened, but do not brown. Remove the pan from the heat and reserve 2 to 3 tablespoons of the oil to brush on the bread.

Place the warm steamed vegetables in a food processor and pulse, adding the warm oil and garlic until it's all a smooth purée. Spoon the purée into a mixing bowl.

Over low heat, warm the cream with the star anise, then strain out the pods. Stir the warmed cream into the purée in the mixing bowl. Season the resulting brandade with salt and white pepper to taste and garnish it with the chopped parsley. Serve it warm with the toasted French bread for dipping.

CHEDDAR WAFERS

BILL CARDWELL, CARDWELL'S AT THE PLAZA AND BC'S KITCHEN

MAKES 24 WAFERS

10 $\frac{1}{2}$ tablespoons butter

$\frac{2}{3}$ pound cheddar, shredded

$\frac{1}{3}$ jalapeño pepper, minced

$\frac{1}{8}$ teaspoon cayenne pepper

$\frac{1}{4}$ tablespoon salt

1 $\frac{1}{3}$ cups flour

2 egg whites

2 cups pecans, toasted and chopped

Using the paddle attachment of your mixer, beat the butter until it's fluffy and light in color. Add the cheese and seasonings. Beat until they're well combined.

Add the flour and mix the dough until it's just combined. Roll it into 8-inch-long cylinders. Brush the cylinders with the egg white and roll them in the pecans to cover. Wrap each cylinder in plastic and freeze it.

Preheat the oven to 325 degrees. Defrost each cylinder, then slice it into 24 pieces. Bake the wafers on a parchment-lined sheet tray for approximately 15 minutes. When done, the wafers should be crisp and easy to pull off of the parchment.

CHORIZO-STUFFED MUSHROOMS

RICHARD BERRI, BOATHOUSE FOREST PARK

MAKES 75 MUSHROOMS

5 pounds button mushrooms

1 onion, peeled and quartered

1 stalk celery, chopped coarsely

2 green peppers, cored, seeded, and chopped

3 pounds Mexican chorizo, casing removed

1 cup butter

2 cups bread crumbs

2 cups Chihuahua cheese, shredded

Separate the mushrooms' tops and stems and reserve the tops. Add the stems to a food processor with the onion, celery, and peppers. Grind till it's smooth.

Brown the chorizo in a skillet, then set it aside in a bowl. In the same skillet, melt the butter and sauté the puréed vegetables in it until most of the liquid is gone, then add the purée to the bowl with the chorizo.

Combine the purée, chorizo, and bread crumbs. Let the mix cool, then stir in the cheese. Roll the final mix into balls and stuff them inside the mushroom tops.

The appetizer can be made ahead of time and refrigerated at this point. Before serving, place the mushrooms in a buttered casserole dish and bake them at 350 degrees until the topping is lightly browned.

LOBSTER RISOTTO
STEVE KOMOREK,
TRATTORIA MARCELLA

SERVES 4

½ small onion, diced

2 teaspoons extra-virgin olive oil

1 tablespoon butter

½ cup assorted mushrooms (shiitake, crimini, oyster), sliced

½ teaspoon garlic, peeled and chopped

½ cup dry white wine

1 cup arborio rice

4 ½ cups lobster stock (or clam juice, diluted with water, 2 parts water to 1 part clam juice)

½ cup tomato sauce

5 ounces lobster meat, cooked

1 cup fresh spinach, washed, stems clipped

½ cup grated Parmigianio-Reggiano

Salt and white pepper

In a medium-size pot with 4-inch-high sides, lightly sauté the onion in the olive oil until it's translucent. Add the butter and mushrooms, and sauté until the mushrooms are soft. Add the chopped garlic. When the garlic is just slightly toasted, add the wine. Let the

liquid reduce by half. Add the arborio rice, one cup of the stock, and the tomato sauce. Continue to stir the rice over a low flame, adding stock as needed, until it has the desired bite and texture, about 20 minutes. When the stock has all been absorbed, at once add the lobster meat, spinach, and Parmigiano-Reggiano. Mix all ingredients and add salt and white pepper to taste.

PIGS UNDER A BLANKET WITH BEER-CHEESE SAUCE
JUSTIN HAIFLEY, THE SHACK
PUBGRUB AND THE TAVERN
KITCHEN & BAR

SERVES 6

4 ½ teaspoons salt

1 tablespoon black pepper

1 tablespoon chili powder

2 tablespoons paprika

1 ½ teaspoons cayenne pepper

1 tablespoon ground cumin

1 teaspoon coriander

6 cloves garlic, roasted

1 ½ teaspoons fresh oregano, minced

1 cup cilantro, minced

2 tablespoons sugar

1 ½ tablespoons tequila

1 ½ tablespoons red-wine vinegar

2 ½ pounds pork shoulder, cut into 1-inch cubes

2 sheets puff pastry

1 egg yolk

1 tablespoon water

In a large bowl, blend together the salt, black pepper, chili powder, paprika, cayenne pepper, cumin, coriander, roasted garlic, oregano, cilantro, sugar, tequila, and red-wine vinegar. Toss the seasonings with the pork. Place the pork on a sheet tray and chill it in the freezer for an hour.

Grind the pork through a meat grinder with a quarter-inch-hole grinder plate or die. Form the ground pork into 1-inch balls. Lay out a sheet of puff pastry on a lightly floured board and cut it into 1 $\frac{1}{2}$–inch squares. Cover each meatball with a square of puff pastry, brush the pastry with egg wash, and place it on a lined sheet pan.

Cook the meatballs in a 350-degree oven for 12 to 15 minutes, until the puff pastry is golden brown and the pork is thoroughly cooked.

BEER-CHEESE SAUCE

MAKES 2 QUARTS

  1 cup onion, diced

  1 teaspoon garlic, minced

  2 tablespoons butter

  2 tablespoons flour

  12 ounces Sofie beer (farmhouse ale)

  1 cup heavy cream

  6 slices American cheese

  1 teaspoon sriracha

  1 tablespoon salt

  4 cups cheddar, shredded

Sauté the onion and garlic in the butter until they're translucent. Whisk in the flour and cook the mixture for 2 minutes. Add the beer and whisk until it's incorporated. Add the cream and heat until it starts to boil. Add the cheese, sriracha, and salt and cook until the cheese is melted. Mix the sauce in a blender until it's smooth and strain it through a fine mesh sieve.

PISTACHIO-CRUSTED HERBED GOAT CHEESE

AARON BAGGETT, EDGEWILD RESTAURANT & WINERY

SERVES 8

$\frac{1}{2}$ cup raw and unsalted pistachios, shelled

4 ounces herbed goat cheese

2 tablespoons quince syrup (see recipe)

Crostini, lavash, or crackers

In a food processor, pulse the pistachios until they're chopped into about a quarter of their original size. Pat the goat cheese into a puck shape and dredge it in the pistachios so it's completely covered.

On a parchment-lined cookie sheet, bake the cheese at 350 degrees for 6 to 8 minutes, or until the cheese is warm. Immediately place it on a serving plate and top it with thesyrup. Serve with *crostini*, lavash, or crackers.

QUINCE SYRUP

  2 cups white wine

  1 cup sugar

  1 quince, diced small

Bring the wine and sugar to a simmer and reduce it by a quarter. Then add the quince and reduce the liquid by another quarter. Let the syrup cool before serving.

Chilled Sesame Noodles

**NY VONGSALY, BAR LES FRÈRES,
BOBO NOODLE HOUSE, AND I FRATTELINI**

SERVES 6

2 tablespoons mushroom
soy sauce

¼ cup Kikkoman soy
sauce

¼ cup sesame oil

1 tablespoon *sambal* chili
sauce

1 teaspoon garlic, minced

3 tablespoons sesame
seeds

2 tablespoons fresh
cilantro, chopped

1 pound capellini

Peanuts, crushed

Fresh cilantro, chopped

Whisk the soy sauces, sesame oil, chili sauce, garlic, sesame seeds, and 2 tablespoons cilantro together in a large mixing bowl. Cook the capellini for 5 to 6 minutes in boiling water. Do not overcook it.

Strain the noodles. Immediately add them to the sauce and toss. Serve the noodles chilled with a garnish of crushed peanuts and chopped cilantro.

SALMON TARTARE WITH EVERYTHING SHORTBREAD

CHRISTOPHER BORK, BLOOD & SAND

SERVES 6

8 ounces fresh salmon, skin removed,
   finely chopped

2 tablespoons fresh lemon juice

1/4 cup flat-leaf parsley, finely chopped

Schmaltz (see recipe)

Kosher salt

Fresh ground black pepper

Everything shortbread pieces (see recipe)

Sesame seeds

SCHMALTZ

1/2 pound chicken fat

1 cup yellow onion, diced

Place the chicken fat in a saucepan on medium heat. When the fat is hot, add the onion, and reduce the heat to low. Slowly cook the mixture, stirring occasionally, until all fat is rendered and the onion is translucent. Strain the resulting schmaltz through a chinois and reserve it at room temperature.

EVERYTHING SHORTBREAD

1 cup butter, room-temperature

1 1/2 tablespoons granulated sugar

1 tablespoon salt

1 3/4 cup flour

2/3 cup cornstarch

1 1/2 tablespoons dried onions

1 tablespoon poppy seeds

1 tablespoon sesame seeds

1/2 teaspoon granulated garlic

Preheat the oven to 350 degrees. Place the butter, sugar, and salt in the bowl of a stand mixer with a paddle attachment. Whip the mixture on medium speed for 2 minutes. Thoroughly combine the rest of the ingredients, then add them to the butter mixture and turn it on low speed. Mix until just combined.

Grease a 12- by 10-inch baking dish. Dump the shortbread mixture into the dish and flatten it out with your hands. Do this quickly, as your hands will melt the butter. Bake the shortbread for 20 minutes, or until it's a light golden brown. Let the shortbread cool, but while it's still very warm, cut it into circles with a 2-inch round biscuit cutter. Remove the pieces from the pan and let them cool on a wire rack.

To serve: Combine the salmon, lemon juice, parsley, and 3 tablespoons of the schmaltz in a bowl and mix thoroughly. Season the mixture with salt and pepper, then place some of it on each piece of everything shortbread. Sprinkle a few sesame seeds on top, then drizzle the tartare with a little more schmaltz.

SMOKED–CHERRY PEPPER WINGS

PETER CLARK, BAILEYS' RANGE AND THE FIFTH WHEEL

MAKES 5 TO 7 DOZEN CHICKEN WINGS

10 red cherry peppers, whole

6 garlic cloves, peeled

1 jalapeño pepper, whole

1 small Spanish onion, peeled and cut into
   1-inch chunks

1 cup cayenne pepper sauce

1/2 cup honey

½ cup butter, softened

5 to 7 dozen chicken wings

Prepare a charcoal grill for grilling, adding wood chips to the coal for extra smoke flavor. Skewer the peppers, garlic cloves, jalapeño, and onion chunks. Place them on the grill rack and cook them until the vegetables are semicharred. Remove the skewers from the heat and let them cool.

When the vegetables are cool enough to handle, remove the stems from the cherry peppers and jalapeño, leaving the peppers intact for intense heat. If less heat is desired, remove some or all of the seeds from the peppers, wearing disposable gloves to protect your hands from the juice. Place all of the vegetables in a blender and process them until smooth. Add the cayenne pepper sauce, honey, and softened butter, then blend until the sauce is uniformly smooth.

Season the chicken wings with salt and pepper and grill them until they're brown and crispy, 15 to 20 minutes, depending on the heat of the grill, turning the wings once in the middle of the cooking time. Once all the wings are grilled, place them in a large bowl and toss them with sauce.

SMOKED SALMON CHIPS

REX HALE, BASSO, THE MARKET AT THE CHESHIRE, THE RESTAURANT AT THE CHESHIRE, AND THREE SIXTY

SERVES 4

½ pound chipotle cream cheese (see recipe)

Homemade Idaho potato chips (see recipe),

or store-bought kettle chips

½ pound hot smoked salmon, flaked (see recipe)

1 red onion, diced

¼ cup capers

2 teaspoons chives, minced

2 tablespoons dry spice mixture (see recipe)

CHIPOTLE CREAM CHEESE

2 tablespoons canned chipotle peppers in adobo sauce

8 ounces cream cheese, room-temperature

¼ cup chives, finely snipped

1 lime, juiced

½ tablespoon kosher salt

½ tablespoon sugar

Place the chipotle peppers in a food processor and purée them until they're smooth. Add the cream cheese and mix well. Add the chives, lime juice, salt, and sugar, and mix. Periodically scrape down the sides of the processor so all ingredients are well-mixed. (This can be prepared up to two days in advance and refrigerated.)

HOT SMOKED SALMON

2 ⅔ cups water

⅜ cup kosher salt

¼ cup caraway seeds

6 tablespoons dark brown sugar

1 cup ice

1 2 ½-pound side of salmon, pin bones removed

To make a brine, combine 1 ⅔ cups of the water with the salt, caraway seeds, and dark brown sugar. Heat the mixture until the salt and sugar are dissolved. Then add the ice. Set the brine aside until the mixture is room-temperature. Place the brine and the fish in a plastic food-storage container and refrigerate it for

18 hours. After 18 hours, remove the salmon from the brine and place it on a sheet pan. Let the uncovered salmon dry overnight in the refrigerator. The next day, place the salmon in a smoker on the roasting rack, with a sheet pan on the bottom to catch the fat. Smoke the meat for two hours in a smoker at a temperature of 150 degrees.

HOMEMADE IDAHO POTATO CHIPS

- 2 Idaho potatoes
- Canola oil
- Dry spice mixture (see recipe)

Heat the canola oil to 300 degrees in a fryer or large pot. Use a mandoline to thinly slice potatoes lengthwise, $1/16$ inch thick. Fry the potatoes on both sides until they're golden brown and crisp, approximately 3 to 5 minutes. Remove them with a skimmer and let them drain on paper towels. Sprinkle the chips with the dry spice mixture.

DRY SPICE MIXTURE

- $1/2$ cup salt
- $1/3$ cup sugar
- $2 \ 1/2$ tablespoons dried thyme
- $1/2$ cup New Mexico chili powder
- $2 \ 1/2$ tablespoons cayenne pepper
- $2 \ 1/2$ tablespoons garlic powder

Mix all of the ingredients together.

To serve: Spread the chipotle cream cheese on the chips. Place a small piece of smoked salmon on top of each chip. Garnish the dish with the red onion, capers, chives, and dry spice seasoning. Serve it immediately.

TAPENADE

REX HALE,
BASSO, THE MARKET AT THE CHESHIRE, THE RESTAURANT AT THE CHESHIRE, AND THREE SIXTY

MAKES 2 QUARTS

- 9 ounces Missouri pecans, toasted
- 6 cups Kalamata olives, pitted
- 3 tablespoons garlic, chopped
- $1/2$ cup capers, drained
- 2 tablespoons lemon zest, minced
- $3/4$ cup extra-virgin olive oil
- Kosher salt
- Finely ground black pepper

Place the pecans, olives, garlic, capers, and lemon zest in a food processor and blend. With the machine running, slowly add the olive oil until the mixture is smooth. Taste and season the tapenade with kosher salt and pepper.

WASABI DEVILED EGGS

DANA HOLLAND,
JILLY'S CUPCAKE BAR & CAFÉ

SERVES 12

2 tablespoons wasabi powder

1 to 2 tablespoons warm water

12 large eggs, hard-boiled

1 scallion, white part minced, green part cut
　into thin rings

1 teaspoon pickled ginger, minced

1/2 tablespoon sesame oil

1/2 teaspoon soy sauce

1/2 cup mayonnaise

Salt

1 to 2 tablespoons toasted mixed black and
　white sesame seeds

2 tablespoons pickled ginger, finely julienned

2 tablespoons tobiko (flying-fish roe),
　wasabi-flavored or plain (optional)

1 tablespoon Huy Fong Foods sriracha
　(optional)

2 tablespoons wasabi sauce (optional, see
　recipe)

In a small bowl, mix the wasabi powder with enough warm water to make a paste. Cover the bowl and set it aside while you prepare the eggs.

Cut the eggs in half lengthwise and pop the yolks into a bowl. Set the whites on a tray or plate, cut side up. Mash the yolks with a fork.

Mix the mashed yolks with half of the wasabi paste, the minced white part of the scallion, minced pickled ginger, sesame oil, soy sauce, and mayonnaise. Blend this mixture well and season it to taste with salt and more wasabi paste. These are normally made pretty peppy, but a mild version is also tasty. All of this may be done a day in advance.

To finish the eggs, sprinkle the toasted sesame seeds on the cut surface of the eggs. Pipe or scoop some of the filling into each egg. Top the filling with a few green-onion rings and a few threads of pickled ginger.

These can be served with a dash of wasabi tobiko and squiggles of sriracha, plus a drizzle of wasabi sauce, for guests to modify their own eggs.

WASABI SAUCE

　1 tablespoon wasabi powder

　1 tablespoon water

　1 tablespoon vegetable oil

Combine all ingredients thoroughly.

Entrées

BEEF MEDALLIONS WITH ARTICHOKE– AND–NIÇOISE OLIVE RELISH

BEN ANDERSON, GIST

SERVES 4

1 ½ pounds beef tenderloin

1 garlic clove, crushed

1 teaspoon thyme, fresh

3 tablespoons extra-virgin olive oil

Kosher salt

Freshly ground black pepper

Niçoise olive relish (see recipe)

Fresh herbs

Cut the tenderloin into 12 equal sections. Pound the beef to flatten it into quarter-inch-thick medallions. Rub the beef with the garlic, sprinkle it with the thyme, then drizzle it with a tablespoon of the olive oil. Cover the beef and let it rest.

Heat a cast-iron skillet over medium-high heat and add the remaining 2 tablespoons of olive oil. Season the beef to taste with the kosher salt and fresh black pepper. Working in batches, cook the beef in the skillet until it's brown on the outside but still pink in the center, about 2 minutes per side. Transfer the beef to a rack and briefly let it rest.

NIÇOISE OLIVE RELISH

1 large red onion, cut into ½-inch slices

6 baby artichokes

½ cup niçoise olives, pitted and coarsely chopped

1 shallot, finely minced

2 tablespoons red-wine vinegar

½ cup extra-virgin olive oil

6 basil sprigs, leaves removed and torn

5 flat-leaf parsley sprigs, leaves removed and torn

5 mint sprigs, leaves removed and torn

½ lemon, zested

Salt and pepper

Preheat the broiler. Place the red onion on a sheet pan and broil it, turning it once, until the slices are charred on both sides, about 4 minutes per side. Let the onion cool, then cut it into quarter-inch cubes.

To blanch the artichokes, trim the tough outer leaves and slice the end of each stem, then cut each artichoke into quarters. Cook the pieces in boiling water until they're tender, 5 to 10 minutes, depending on the size of the artichokes.

In a nonreactive bowl, combine the onion, artichoke, niçoise olives, shallot, red-wine vinegar, extra-virgin olive oil, basil, parsley, mint, and lemon zest. Toss the mixture well to combine it, and add salt and pepper to taste.

To serve: Arrange the beef on four plates and spoon the niçoise olive relish over the top. Garnish the dish with additional fresh herbs.

Note: This works well with smashed potatoes.

BISON MEATLOAF

D. SCOTT PHILLIPS, BALABAN'S WINE CELLAR & TAPAS BAR

SERVES 8

2 pounds ground bison

3 garlic cloves, minced

2 eggs, lightly beaten

1 cup raw bacon, finely chopped

1 small sweet onion, minced

1/2 cup panko

1/2 cup grated Manchego cheese

1 tablespoon Worcestershire sauce

2 teaspoons kosher salt

1 teaspoon dried sage

1 teaspoon dried basil

1 teaspoon dried oregano

Vegetable oil

Chef D. Scott's Favorite Meatloaf Sauce (see recipe)

Preheat the oven to 350 degrees. Place all of the ingredients except the oil and meatloaf sauce together in a large bowl and mix them with your hands. Coat a small casserole dish with the oil. Pat the mixture into the pan in a loaf shape. Cover the pan with aluminum foil. Bake the meatloaf for 1 1/2 hours, then drizzle the top with the meatloaf sauce.

CHEF D. SCOTT'S FAVORITE MEATLOAF SAUCE

1 cup ketchup

1/2 cup apple cider

3/4 cup brown sugar

2 tablespoons mustard

1 teaspoon kosher salt

Whisk together the ketchup, cider, sugar, mustard, and kosher salt in a saucepan and warm it to melt the sugar.

BLOWTORCH RIBS

SCOTT THOMAS, GRILLIN' FOOLS

SERVES 6 TO 8

1 quart apple juice

1/4 cup salt

2 tablespoons garlic, minced

1 teaspoon fresh cracked black pepper

2 slabs baby back ribs

2 tablespoons granulated garlic

2 tablespoons turbinado or raw sugar

2 tablespoons pumpkin-pie spice

1 tablespoon sweet paprika

2 tablespoons apple jelly

2 tablespoons apricot preserves

2 tablespoons hot-pepper jelly

2 teaspoons Worcestershire sauce

To brine the ribs, combine the apple juice, salt, minced garlic, and black pepper in a resealable plastic bag and slosh it around until the salt is dissolved. Remove the membrane from the back of the ribs, place them in the bag with the brine, and refrigerate them overnight.

To make the rub, combine the granulated garlic, turbinado, pumpkin-pie spice, and sweet paprika in a bowl. Give the bone side of the ribs between a dusting and a coating of the rub, to your preference. Flip the ribs and repeat on the meat side.

Prepare the grill for two-zone grilling (or indirect grilling), with coals and smoke wood on one side and nothing on the other. The target temperature of the inside of the grill is 275 to 300 degrees. Place the ribs on the side of the grill with no heat and close the lid.

To make the glaze, combine the apple jelly, apricot preserves, hot-pepper jelly, and Worcestershire sauce in a bowl and put it in the microwave for about 90 seconds to liquefy the gelatin and allow the ingredients to combine. Mix them together well. When the meat on the grill pulls back from the bone about a half-inch, which should take about 2 hours at this temperature, flip the slabs over to the bone side and slather them with the glaze.

CONTINUED ON PG. 82

Sweet Tea–Brined Pork Tenderloin With Sweet-Corn Pudding and Apple-Bacon Chutney

CASSY VIRES, HOME WINE KITCHEN AND TABLE
SERVES 4

PORK TENDERLOIN

¼ cup kosher salt

¾ cup sugar

8 ounces loose-leaf black
  tea leaves

2 cups boiling water

3 cups ice cubes

2 1-pound pork tenderloins

2 tablespoons olive oil

Salt and pepper

SWEET-CORN PUDDING

5 tablespoons unsalted
  butter

½ cup all-purpose flour

1 ½ teaspoons sugar

1 teaspoon salt

1 ¾ cup milk

3 large eggs

4 cups fresh corn kernels

Butter

Salt and pepper

APPLE-BACON CHUTNEY

6 strips hickory-smoked
  bacon, chopped

1 large onion, diced

2 Gala apples, diced

1 teaspoon fresh thyme

¼ cup apple cider

Salt and pepper

Preheat the oven to 425 degrees. Combine the salt, sugar, and tea leaves in a heat-proof bowl. Pour over the boiling water, stir, and let steep for 10 minutes. Add the ice and stir to cool.

Once the tea is cool to the touch, add the pork tenderloins and refrigerate 30 to 60 minutes. Remove the pork from the brine, rinse well, and pat dry with paper towels.

Place a large stainless-steel skillet over high heat. Season the pork tenderloins and sear on all sides in the olive oil. Place the skillet into the oven to finish cooking, about 10 minutes. Cook the pork until the internal temperature reads 140 degrees. Set aside to rest for 15 minutes before slicing.

Preheat the oven to 375 degrees. In a medium saucepan, melt the butter and whisk in the flour, sugar, and salt. Cook over moderately high heat for 1 minute. Gradually whisk in the milk and cook over medium heat until the sauce thickens, about 4 minutes. In a medium bowl, beat the eggs. Temper the sauce into the egg mixture. Fold in the corn and season the pudding with salt and pepper.

Butter a 9-inch cast-iron skillet and pour in the corn mixture. Bake for 30 minutes or until it's cooked through and lightly brown on top.

Place a large nonstick skillet over medium heat and cook the bacon until crispy. Remove the bacon with a slotted spoon, leaving the grease in the pan. Sauté the onion in the bacon fat until soft and translucent, but not yet brown. Return the bacon to the pan and add the apples, thyme, and apple cider. Cook for about 20 minutes, or until thickened and reduced. Season to taste and serve with the pan-roasted pork tenderloin and corn pudding.

Blast the glaze with a blowtorch for a couple of minutes, making sure the flame is blue and not orange (so the fuel is fully burning), constantly rocking the flame slowly back and forth across the glaze. Flip the slabs over to the meat side and smear it with the glaze, then blast it with the torch in the same manner. Once a sugary crust is achieved on all the slabs, remove them from the heat, let them rest for 5 minutes, slice them, and serve.

CACIO E PEPE

GERARD CRAFT, BRASSERIE BY
NICHE, NICHE, PASTARIA, AND TASTE

SERVES 1

Salted water

6 ounces pasta, such as egg tagliolini,
    bucatini, or spaghetti

1/4 cup pasta water

Fresh cracked pepper

2 tablespoons butter

2 ounces Pecorino Romano, grated

Cook the pasta in boiling salted water. In a sauté pan, add 1/4 cup of the pasta water, pepper to taste, and the butter. Bring the liquid to a boil to emulsify the butter. When the pasta is cooked, drain it and add it to the butter/pepper mix. Toss the pasta to coat it and add the cheese. Adjust the sauce's consistency with pasta water as necessary.

CASSOULET WITH DUCK AND PORK BELLY

JOHN PERKINS,
ENTRE

SERVES 4 TO 6

1 1/2 cups dry white beans, such as cannellini

Thyme, bay leaf, rosemary, and sage, tied into
    a bouquet garni

1 onion, halved and studded with a few whole
    cloves

1/4 pound smoked pork belly (can substitute
    bacon)

1 1/2 cup red wine

2 to 3 tablespoons tomato paste

Salt and white pepper

1 cup bread crumbs

1 1/2 cup duck fat (or butter), melted

3 pieces of duck confit, with thigh and leg
    (available at Straub's)

Cover the dry beans with water and soak them overnight. Drain them the next day, then bring the beans to a simmer in enough cold water to cover them by about an inch. Add the bouquet garni, onion halves, and smoked pork belly or bacon. Bring the water to a boil for a few minutes before turning it down.

Let the beans simmer for approximately 1 hour, or until they're cooked, but not mushy. The water will evaporate, but make sure the beans stay covered. Discard the onion, herbs, and pork. Add the red wine and tomato paste, and continue to cook the beans for another half hour. Season the beans with salt and white pepper to taste.

Blend the melted duck fat (or butter) with the bread crumbs. Place the duck confit in a large casserole or cast-iron pan and pour the beans over the top. Top it all with the bread-crumb mixture, patting it down to help form a crust on top.

Bake the cassoulet in the oven at 375 degrees for 15 to 20 minutes, or until the bread crumbs begin to brown.

CHAR SIU PORK STEAKS

JUSTIN HAIFLEY,
THE SHACK PUBGRUB AND
TAVERN KITCHEN & BAR

SERVES 6 TO 8

CHAR SIU

3 tablespoons maltose (available at most Asian grocery stores)

3 tablespoons honey

3 tablespoons hoisin sauce

3 tablespoons sweet soy sauce

1 teaspoon Chinese five-spice powder

1 teaspoon white pepper

2 tablespoons sesame oil

8 cloves garlic, peeled and sliced

Combine all the ingredients in a small saucepan and simmer them over medium heat until the maltose and honey are melted and the sauce is slightly thickened. Let it cool completely.

BRINE

1 quart water

½ teaspoon curing salt

½ cup brown sugar

3 tablespoons kosher salt

1 apple, diced

½ onion, diced

1 stalk celery, diced

1 teaspoon allspice berries

2 cloves

1 cinnamon stick

2 star anise

6 cloves garlic

12 peppercorns

6 bay leaves

2 pounds pork butt, cut into 4 pieces

Place all the ingredients except the pork into a large pot and bring it to a simmer until the salt and sugar have dissolved. Let it chill completely. Marinate the pork steaks in the brine for 48 hours. Remove them from the brine and pat them dry.

Brush the pork with generous amounts of char siu marinade. Let it marinate for several hours.

Grill the steaks on both sides until heated through.

CHAUMETTE CHICKEN

ADAM LAMBAY,
CHAUMETTE VINEYARDS & WINERY

SERVES 4

CHICKEN

¼ cup olive oil

4 garlic cloves, peeled and minced

1 tablespoon kosher salt or sea salt

½ teaspoon pepper

1 tablespoon fresh thyme, chopped

1 teaspoon fresh rosemary, chopped

3 tablespoons fresh Italian or curly-leaf parsley, chopped

1 5-pound chicken, split and quartered

Heat a large roasting pan over medium heat. Separately, blend together the olive oil, minced garlic, salt, pepper,

CONTINUED ON PG. 86

SqWires Chicken Pot Pie and Puff Pastry

BETHANY BUDDE, SQWIRES

SERVES 6

1 whole, fresh, free-range
chicken

¼ cup olive oil

Salt and pepper

2 large tomatoes

1 cup sweet peas

1 large yellow onion

1 zucchini or squash

6 small new red potatoes

1 tablespoon fresh garlic

½ cup white wine

3 cups chicken or vegetable
stock

1 ½ cups corn off the cob

¾ cup fresh herbs of your
choice (such as a mix
of rosemary, flat pars-
ley, sage, and oregano),
chopped

1 sheet of puff pastry, cut
into 6 squares

Clean and rub chicken with 2 tablespoons of the olive oil and salt and pepper. Cover and roast at 325 degrees for 1 hour and 15 minutes. Let cool. Pull the white and dark meat off the bones and discard the skin.

While the chicken is cooking, chop and purée the tomatoes. Also, dice the onion, squash, and new potatoes.

Sauté onion in 2 tablespoons of the olive oil. Add garlic and sauté until fragrant. Add the pulled chicken and white wine. Let wine reduce. Add the puréed tomatoes, zucchini, potatoes, corn, and the herbs. Pour in the stock and simmer uncovered for 45 minutes, until the filling thickens and the potatoes are tender. Add salt and pepper to taste.

Place the puff pastry on a lined sheet pan and bake in a 325-degree oven for 12 to 15 minutes, or until brown and flaky.

Ladle the soup into deep bowls and top with the flaky puff pastry.

thyme, rosemary, and parsley. Coat the chicken pieces with the oil mixture. Place the chicken in the hot roasting pan. Generously brown both sides of the meat and remove it from the pan.

BRAISE

- 4 tablespoons butter
- 1/2 pound thick-cut bacon, diced
- 1 large yellow or white onion, julienned
- 1/2 cup fresh garlic, chopped
- 2 cups quartered crimini mushrooms (or your personal favorite)
- 1 teaspoon fresh thyme, chopped
- 1/2 teaspoon fresh rosemary, chopped
- 2 tablespoons fresh Italian parsley, chopped
- 1 1/2 cups Chaumette Chambourcin wine
- 1 bay leaf
- 1 quart chicken stock
- 1 pound new red potatoes, sliced
- 1 turnip, peeled and sliced
- Salt and pepper

Add the butter to the pan, then add the bacon. Brown the bacon. With a wooden spoon, scrape the bottom of the pan.

Add the onion and sauté it until it's translucent but not brown. Add the chopped garlic. When the edges of the onions start to brown, add the mushrooms and herbs. Continue to cook the mushrooms until all the moisture evaporates. When the pan is dry, deglaze it with the Chaumette Chambourcin. Bring the wine to a boil and let it reduce by at least half.

Preheat the oven to 350 degrees. Return the chicken to the pan, skin side up. Add the bay leaf and the chicken stock. Bring the liquid to a boil, then drop in the potato and turnip slices. Place the pan in the oven and let it roast uncovered for about an hour, or until the legs are fork-tender. Remove the pan from the oven.

Remove the chicken from the pan. Bring the sauce back to a boil. Reduce it to the desired consistency. Add salt and pepper to taste.

CHICKEN ADOBO

BRIAN HARDESTY, ELEMENT AND GUERILLA STREET FOOD
SERVES 6

- 2 cups jasmine rice
- 2 cups water
- 1 cup soy sauce
- 1 cup coconut or cider vinegar
- 8 whole garlic cloves
- 1 tablespoon whole black peppercorns
- 3 bay leaves
- 2 pounds boneless, skinless chicken thighs
- 1/4 cup coconut milk
- 1/4 cup cold water
- 1 tablespoon cornstarch
- Fresh scallions, chopped

Simmer the jasmine rice in 2 cups of water for 20 minutes. Cover the rice and turn the heat down to low.

Combine the soy sauce, vinegar, garlic, black peppercorns, and bay leaves in a large pot and bring it to a boil. Add the whole chicken thighs and simmer them until they're fork-tender, about 40 minutes. Add the coconut milk and simmer the chicken for an additional 10 minutes.

Mix the cold water with the cornstarch. Slowly whisk the cornstarch mixture into the pot until the liquid thickens to a gravy-like consistency.

Remove the bay leaves before serving. Serve the chicken adobo over the rice and garnish it with the chopped scallions.

CHICKEN PISTACHIO

RICH LoRUSSO, LoRUSSO'S CUCINA

SERVES 4

Olive oil

4 6-ounce boneless, skinless chicken breasts

1 cup pistachios, finely chopped

1/2 cup sweet onion, minced

1/4 cup brandy

1 cup peach nectar

1/2 cup peach preserves

Fresh black pepper

1 cup peach slices, fresh or frozen

1/4 cup sun-dried cherries

1 split (6 ounces) sparkling wine

1 teaspoon cornstarch (optional)

1 teaspoon cold water (optional)

Preheat the oven to 200 degrees. Lightly oil the chicken breasts and dredge them in the chopped pistachios. Add 2 tablespoons of oil to a large frying pan and sauté the chicken breasts over medium heat for 2 minutes, or until they're nicely browned. Turn the chicken over and cook it 2 minutes more, then place it in an oven-safe pan in the oven.

Drain any excess fat from the frying pan and sauté the onion until it's lightly browned. With the pan off the flame, slowly add the brandy, and let it flame up. Be careful. Add the peach nectar and peach preserves. Season the sauce with a few turns of fresh black pepper. Cook it on medium-low heat until it's slightly thickened, about 4 minutes.

Add the peaches and the sun-dried cherries (plus more to taste if desired) and warm them. Top them with the sparkling wine, then place the chicken back in the sauce. If a thicker sauce is desired, mix 1 teaspoon cornstarch and 1 teaspoon cold water, then whisk it

into the sauce. Cook the sauce until it's the desired consistency, then serve the dish.

CHICKEN WITH MOLE SAUCE

JASON TILFORD,
BARRISTER'S IN CLAYTON, MILAGRO
MODERN MEXICAN, MISSION TACO
JOINT, TORTILLARIA MEXICAN KITCHEN

SERVES 6 TO 8

1 whole chicken

2 tablespoons sea salt

Mole sauce (see recipe)

2 cups water or chicken stock

1/4 cup toasted sesame seeds

Preheat the oven to 425 degrees. Clean and rinse the chicken. Pat it dry and season it with the sea salt. Let it stand for 5 minutes, then rub it with 1 cup of the mole sauce. Place the chicken in a roasting pan and cook it uncovered for 20 minutes. Remove it from the oven, add 2 cups of water or chicken stock, and cover it with foil. Place it back in the oven, cook it for 45 minutes more, and remove it. Let it rest for 10 minutes, then carve it and serve it topped with more mole sauce and some toasted sesame seeds.

MOLE SAUCE

MAKES 1 1/2 QUARTS

4 poblano peppers

8 ancho chili peppers, toasted, stemmed, and seeded

4 Guajillo chili peppers, toasted, stemmed, and seeded

CONTINUED ON PG. 90

**JIM VOSS,
OVERLOOK FARM
AND NATHALIE'S**

**What is your must-have
spice?** *Herbes de* Provence.

One great cooking tip?
Learn more from your mis-
takes than your successes.

**Your favorite five-ingre-
dient dish?** Green gaz-
pacho: cucumber, kale,
cilantro, jalapeño, and lime.

**What's your favorite
comfort food?** *Osso buco*
Milanese.

Sangria Chicken

JIM VOSS, OVERLOOK FARM AND NATHALIE'S

SERVES 4

SANGRIA BUTTER SAUCE

- ½ cup white wine
- ½ cup chicken stock
- 1 tablespoon shallot, minced
- 1 tablespoon lemon juice
- 1 teaspoon orange zest
- 2 tablespoons Chambord liqueur
- ½ cup heavy cream
- ½ cup butter, diced

4 chicken breasts

MARINADE

- ¼ cup chopped parsley
- 1 tablespoon chopped garlic
- 1 tablespoon *herbes de Provence*
- 1 tablespoon Dijon mustard
- ¼ cup olive oil
- 1 tablespoon lemon juice
- 1 teaspoon kosher salt
- ½ teaspoon fresh black pepper

SANGRIA BUTTER SAUCE

In a saucepan, combine the wine, stock, shallot, lemon juice, orange zest, and Chambord. Bring to a boil and reduce by half. Add cream and reduce by half again. On low heat, whisk in the cold butter. Keep warm.

MARINADE

Whisk together the parsley, garlic, herbs, mustard, oil, lemon juice, salt, and pepper. Rub the mixture over the chicken breasts. Let the chicken marinate for 30 minutes at room temperature, or for 3 to 4 hours in the refrigerator. Bring the chicken back to room temperature before cooking it. Charbroil or roast it in a 375-degree oven for 15 minutes.

PEACH SALSA

- 6 peaches, peeled and diced
- 1 red onion, sliced and diced small
- 1 red bell pepper, diced small
- 1 teaspoon lime juice
- 1 teaspoon chopped cilantro
- 1 teaspoon fresh mint, chopped
- ½ teaspoon salt
- 1 pinch cayenne pepper

Toss together the peaches, onion, pepper, lime juice, herbs, salt, and cayenne.

To serve: Present the chicken on a pool of sangria butter sauce and top it with the peach salsa.

3 garlic cloves, chopped

4 cups low-sodium chicken broth

1/2 cup almonds

1/4 cup peanuts

1/4 cup raisins

2 whole cloves

1 tablespoon kosher salt

1 teaspoon cinnamon

2 tablespoons sugar

2 ounces Mexican chocolate

2 cups tomatoes, diced

On a gas grill or broiler, roast the poblano peppers until their skin is blistered and slightly black in spots. Wrap them in plastic wrap and let them sit for 10 minutes. Remove the wrap and skin the peppers. Then slice them in half and remove the seeds and stem. In a large saucepan, combine the poblano, ancho, and Guajillo chili peppers with the garlic, chicken broth, nuts, raisins, cloves, salt, cinnamon, sugar, Mexican chocolate, and diced tomatoes and bring it to a boil. Reduce the heat to a simmer and cook it for 30 to 40 minutes.

Remove the saucepan from the heat and let the contents cool slightly so they're a safe temperature to blend. Blend the sauce in small batches until it's smooth, then return it to the stovetop. Cook it for another 5 to 10 minutes, adjusting the viscosity as needed with more broth or warm water.

CIDER-BRAISED BEEF BRISKET

BILL CARDWELL, CARDWELL'S AT THE PLAZA AND BC'S KITCHEN

SERVES 6

1 tablespoon kosher salt

1 tablespoon black pepper

1 tablespoon Hungarian paprika

1 tablespoon granulated garlic

1 tablespoon fresh thyme, chopped

5 pounds brisket, flat-end, trimmed, excess fat reserved

1/2 cup vegetable oil

4 extra-large yellow onions, peeled and sliced thin

2 carrots, peeled and shredded

1/4 cup garlic, peeled and minced

1 cup apple-cider vinegar

2 cups fresh apple cider

4 cups low-sodium beef broth

1 cup ketchup

Salt and pepper

Preheat the oven to 350 degrees. Mix together the kosher salt, pepper, paprika, granulated garlic, and chopped thyme. Rub both sides of the brisket with the seasonings. Heat the vegetable oil in a large skillet or Dutch oven, large enough to accommodate the meat. Brown it well on both sides.

Place the browned meat in a roasting pan. In the skillet with the drippings from browning the meat, add the onions, carrots, and minced garlic. Cook the vegetables until they're soft and golden.

Add the apple-cider vinegar, cider, beef broth, and ketchup to the browned vegetables and bring the liquid to a boil. Pour the mixture over the meat. If there isn't enough liquid to cover the meat, add more beef broth.

Cover the roasting pan with a tight-fitting lid or with foil and bake the brisket until it's tender, or approximately 1 1/2 to 2 hours. Allow the meat to rest in its juices for 30 to 40 minutes before serving it.

Remove the meat from the pan and cover it to keep it warm. Skim the fat from the juices and place the juices and vegetable solids in a food processor or blender. Pulse to blend them. Season the sauce with salt and pepper to taste. Cut the cooked meat across the grain into thin slices. Ladle the sauce over the meat and serve.

CRISPY RED SNAPPER WITH SHRIMP AND CLEAR CREOLE BROTH

REX HALE, BASSO, THE MARKET AT THE CHESHIRE, THE RESTAURANT AT THE CHESHIRE, THREE SIXTY

SERVES 3

2 teaspoons vegetable oil

6 6- to 7-ounce red snapper fillets, skin on

Salt and pepper

3 cups clear Creole broth (see recipe)

12 16- to 20-count shrimp, peeled, deveined, and chopped

1 serrano pepper, seeded and sliced thin

2 tablespoons yellow onion, julienned into 1-inch slices

2 tablespoons leek, julienned into 1-inch slices

2 tablespoons celery, julienned into 1-inch slices

2 tablespoons yellow bell pepper, julienned into 1-inch slices

4 teaspoons fresh basil leaves, cut into a chiffonade

2 teaspoons fresh thyme leaves, chopped

Place a large nonstick skillet over high heat and add the vegetable oil. Season the fillets with salt and pepper to taste. Place the snapper fillets in the skillet, skin side down. Cook them until the skin is very crisp, about 3 minutes. Turn the fish over and cook it for an additional 2 minutes.

CLEAR CREOLE BROTH (MAKES 3 CUPS)

1 medium yellow onion, peeled and chopped

2 stalks celery, cleaned and chopped

1 green bell pepper, seeded and chopped

1 serrano pepper, seeded and chopped

4 cloves garlic, peeled

10 medium tomatoes, chopped

Place all of the ingredients in a large blender. Blend the mixture until it's smooth. Place it in an 8-quart saucepan over high heat. Bring it to a boil, then turn the temperature down and let it simmer for 5 minutes. Line a fine mesh strainer with damp heavy cloth. Pour the mixture into the strainer and let the clear liquid drain into a container.

To serve: Pour the Creole broth into a 2-quart saucepan over high heat and bring it to a simmer. Add the shrimp, serrano pepper, onion, leek, celery, bell pepper, basil, and thyme to the broth.

Check the seasoning. Ladle the broth with vegetables and shrimp into large soup plates. On each plate, lay two snapper fillets skin-side-up on top of the broth and vegetables.

Boathouse Shrimp Boil and Rémoulade

RICHARD BERRI, BOATHOUSE FOREST PARK

SERVES 10

3 quarts water

3 quarts Schlafly American pale ale

1 lemon

2 bay leaves

1 6-ounce can Old Bay seasoning

1 onion, quartered

1/2 cup garlic powder

1/2 cup paprika

1 tablespoon cayenne pepper

5 pounds U-12 shrimp

Rémoulade (see recipe)

In a large pot, combine the water, beer, lemon, bay leaves, Old Bay seasoning, onion, and spices, and bring the liquid to a rolling boil. Drop the shrimp in and cook them for 4 to 5 minutes, or until they're firm and pink. Strain the liquid and set it aside. Serve the shrimp with the rémoulade.

RÉMOULADE

1/2 cup onion

1 roasted red pepper

2 cloves garlic, peeled

4 cups mayonnaise

1/4 cup sweet chili sauce

1/2 cups capers, drained

In a food processor, grind the onion, roasted red pepper, and garlic until it's a smooth paste. In a mixing bowl, combine the paste with the mayonnaise and sweet chili sauce. Pulse the capers four or five times in the food processor, then mix them into the sauce.

DUCK BREAST WITH DATE PURÉE, PARSNIPS, AND CHORIZO VINAIGRETTE

PATRICK CONNOLLY, BASSO

SERVES 4

4 duck breasts

1 teaspoon thyme, chopped

1 teaspoon rosemary, chopped

Salt and pepper

2 tablespoons honey

1 tablespoon hazelnuts, chopped

Date purée (see recipe)

Parsnips (see recipe)

Chorizo vinaigrette (see recipe)

Using the tip of a sharp knife, score the skin of the duck breasts. Toss them with the thyme and rosemary, and season both sides with salt and pepper.

Heat a pan over medium heat and place the duck breasts in it, skin side down. Render the meat for about 10 minutes, continually draining the rendered fat and pressing on the meat to help the skin crisp. When the skin has rendered well and is a nice caramel color, flip the meat, and continue to cook the flesh side for another 4 minutes.

Turn off the heat and leave the duck in the pan to rest. Spread the honey onto the skin and sprinkle the chopped hazelnuts on top.

DATE PURÉE

1 cup Medjool dates, pitted

1 ½ cups white wine

1 tablespoon coriander seeds, toasted, in a sachet

Place the dates in a pot and cover them with the wine. Add the coriander-seed sachet and cook the dates on medium-high heat for 15 minutes, or until they're tender and beginning to fall apart. Remove the sachet and purée the dates in a food processor.

PARSNIPS

2 tablespoons extra-virgin olive oil

4 medium parsnips, cut into short batons

Salt and pepper

1 tablespoon butter

2 teaspoons fresh thyme, chopped

In a sauté pan, heat the extra-virgin olive oil on high until it ripples. Add the parsnips in a single layer and roast them without moving them for 1 minute. Season them to taste with salt and pepper and toss them once or twice. Add the butter and thyme, cook the parsnips for an additional minute, and remove them from the heat.

CHORIZO VINAIGRETTE

4 ounces Mexican chorizo

1 shallot, minced

2 teaspoons maple syrup

1 tablespoon sherry vinegar

Remove the chorizo from its casing and heat the crumbles in a pan over medium-high heat for 5 minutes. Add the shallot and sweat it for 3 minutes. Add the maple syrup and sherry vinegar and turn off the heat.

To serve: Spread some of the date purée onto each plate. Spoon parsnips onto the purée. Slice the duck and shingle it on top of the parsnips. Spoon a small amount of the chorizo vinaigrette around each plate.

DUCK-CONFIT POT PIE

ALLY NISBET, THE SHAVED DUCK

SERVES 12

DUCK CONFIT

4 cups sugar

4 cups kosher salt

1 teaspoon curing salt

¼ cup peppercorn blend

8 cloves garlic

6 bay leaves, crushed

4 fresh duck-leg quarters

1 quart duck fat (available at Kitchen
Conservatory and Straub's)

Mix the sugar, salts, pepper, garlic, and bay leaves
and apply an even coat of the mix over the duck legs.
Cover and cure for 18 to 36 hours in the refrigerator.
Rinse. Preheat oven to 350 degrees.

Place duck legs on a sheet pan and bake in the oven
for 25 minutes. Transfer to a deep hotel pan, cover with
duck fat, and cook for 1 hour. After an hour, reduce heat
to 250 degrees and cook for another 4 to 6 hours. Strain
duck fat and save for another batch.

POT PIE

6 tablespoons butter

¼ cup flour

1 quart heavy cream

2 onions, chopped fine

4 stalks celery, diced medium

3 carrots, diced medium

1 cup fresh corn off the cob

2 cups green beans

2 teaspoons sage

2 teaspoons cardamom

1 tablespoon black pepper

1 tablespoon celery salt

1 tablespoon kosher salt

1 tablespoon garlic

2 tablespoons sriracha sauce

4 duck confit legs, meat removed and
shredded

1 package high-quality puff pastry, made with
butter

Melt 4 tablespoons of the butter and add the flour.
Continue to cook the roux over very low heat for
5 minutes, or until it reaches a nice blond color. Warm
the cream and slowly add it to the roux. Whisk it
continuously until it thickens.

In a separate pan, melt the remaining 2 tablespoons
of butter and sweat the onions, celery, and carrots. Add
the corn and green beans. Add the seasonings, sriracha,
roux, and duck. Simmer gently for 30 minutes.

Defrost the puff pastry. Preheat oven to 350 degrees.

Turn a heat-proof bowl over and cut the puff pastry
an inch or so larger than the diameter. Ladle the pot-pie
mixture into the cup or bowl and place the puff pastry
on top, pressing down the sides of the bowl. Bake the
pot pie in the oven for 10 minutes, or until the puff
pastry has risen to a nice, flaky texture.

DUCK MEATBALLS/
DUCK BURGERS

PETER CLARK, BAILEYS' RANGE
AND THE FIFTH WHEEL

MAKES 20 MEATBALLS OR 4 BURGER PATTIES

1 pound ground duck, including skin

½ cup orange juice

2 eggs

1 tablespoon ground ginger

1 tablespoon crushed red pepper

2 teaspoons chopped garlic

2 teaspoon chopped scallions

1 teaspoon soy sauce

1 teaspoon teriyaki sauce

1 teaspoon black pepper

1/2 teaspoon kosher salt

1 1/2 cup bread crumbs

Vegetable oil

Combine the ground duck with all the ingredients except the bread crumbs and vegetable oil. Mix well. Add the bread crumbs 1/2 cup at a time, mixing well after each addition. Portion the duck into golf ball–size meatballs. Place them on an oiled sheet pan and bake them in a 325-degree oven for 10 to 15 minutes, until they are just cooked through.

BURGERS

4 hamburger buns

2 tablespoons melted butter

4 butter-lettuce leaves

1 tomato, sliced

4 duck eggs (available through Eat Here
    St. Louis, 314-518-6074, eatherestl.com)

This recipe can be made into full-size burgers by simply grilling 6-ounce portions of the duck mixture. Brush each bun with melted butter and quickly grill it. Top each bun with a duck burger, butter lettuce, fresh tomato, and a duck egg cooked sunny side up.

FILET "DUCK DINER STYLE" WITH DRUNKEN OAT RISOTTO; MAPLE, SORGHUM, AND BOURBON HOLLANDAISE; AND FRIED DUCK EGG

NICK ZOTOS, MIKE SHANNON'S
STEAKS & SEAFOOD

SERVES 2

1 8-ounce grass-fed filet mignon

Kosher salt

Black pepper, finely ground

4 eggs

1 1/2 cups clarified butter

1 tablespoon cayenne pepper

1 tablespoon kosher salt

1/4 cup high-quality bourbon

1/4 cup sorghum

1/4 cup maple syrup

3 strips applewood-smoked bacon

2 duck eggs (available from Eat Here
    St. Louis)

2 tablespoons grape-seed oil

3 tablespoons butter

1/2 garlic clove, minced

1/2 leek, sliced and cleaned

1/2 cup onions, finely diced

3/4 cups white wine

1/2 cup Michelob AmberBock beer

1/2 cup high-quality bourbon

2 cups Irish oats

3 cups chicken stock

3/4 cup Parmesan

Sliced green onions

Heavily season the filet mignon with salt and pepper. Grill or sear to desired temperature. Let rest 5 minutes before serving.

Separate the four egg yolks from the egg whites. Whisk together the egg yolks in a stainless-steel bowl set over a pan with simmering water until the eggs have slightly thickened.

Away from the heat, slowly whisk in the clarified butter. Season with cayenne pepper and kosher salt. Reserve and keep warm, but do not let it get too hot.

Place the bourbon in a pan on the stove. Carefully reduce the bourbon, as the alcohol might ignite. Burn off the alcohol, approximately 3 minutes. Add the sorghum and maple syrup and reduce for 5 to 10 minutes. Remove from the heat and cool. Fold $^1/_2$ tablespoon of the reduction into the hollandaise.

Fry the bacon until crisp, then drain the grease.

Heat a skillet. Add a small amount of oil. Place a 1-inch-high ring mold into the center of the pan. Crack each duck egg into the ring mold. Fry it until the white starts to set or until desired doneness. Set eggs aside.

In another pan, melt the butter on medium-low heat and sauté the garlic, leek, and onion, but do not brown. Deglaze with the white wine. Reduce the wine until almost dry. Add the bourbon and beer and cook until reduced by half. Add the oats. Cook until the liquid is almost absorbed. Add the stock. Cook the sauce until it's creamy. Stir in the cheese and season it.

To serve: Place the oats on the center of the plate. Top with the filet. Crosshatch the three strips of bacon on top of the filet. Next, gently place the duck egg on top of the bacon, but be careful not to puncture the egg yolk. Pour the hollandaise over the top and garnish it with green onion.

GRILLED HERITAGE HOG RIB CHOP WITH SUMMER FRUIT GINGER CHUTNEY AND FRIED POTATOES

LOU ROOK III, ANNIE GUNN'S

SERVES 6

3 16-ounce rib or loin pork chops

Kosher salt

Fresh black pepper

Granulated garlic

Extra-virgin olive oil

Dried basil (optional)

Summer fruit ginger chutney (see recipe)

Remove chops from refrigerator and allow to come to room temperature. Fire up the grill, and when hot, clean and season grill. Season the chops generously with kosher salt, pepper, and granulated garlic on each side. Rub each side with olive oil. If desired, sprinkle dried basil on top. Grill on medium-high heat (400 degrees) for 15 minutes per side to sear the meat. Grill to an internal temperature of 142 degrees and let pork rest for a minimum of 10 minutes before carving or serving it.

SUMMER FRUIT GINGER CHUTNEY

SERVES 20

VANILLA-WINE SYRUP

2 cups dry white wine

$^1/_2$ cup white-wine vinegar

1 cup granulated sugar

$^1/_2$ cup honey

1 vanilla bean, split lengthwise

2 teaspoons red-pepper flakes

8 whole cloves

Basil stems

CONTINUED ON PG. 100

PAUL MANNO, PAUL MANNO'S CAFE

Who taught you to cook? My grandmother and my mother.

What's your favorite cookbook? *The Silver Spoon.*

What's your favorite comfort food? A beautiful plate of simple pasta on a Sunday afternoon.

Rigatoni Arrabbiata "Angry Man's Pasta"

PAUL MANNO, PAUL MANNO'S CAFÉ

SERVES 3 TO 4

2 16-ounce cans San Marzano tomatoes (Poma Rosa, if you can find them)

1 tablespoon salt

2 tablespoons black pepper

1/3 cup extra-virgin olive oil

8 to 10 medium to large fresh basil leaves, torn into pieces

6 cloves fresh garlic, minced medium

1 tablespoon unsalted butter

2 cups button mushrooms, sliced

1/3 cup capers

1 teaspoon crushed red-pepper flakes (or 3 teaspoons if you want it hot)

1/2 cup green and black Kalamata olives, pitted and sliced

2 anchovy fillets (optional)

1/4 cup chardonnay or pinot grigio

Water

1 pound De Cecco rigatoni

2 handfuls Parmigiano-Reggiano, grated

2 whole fresh basil leaves

Use a food mill to crush the tomatoes directly into a stockpot. Add salt and pepper, and cook on medium heat.

In a separate sauté pan, heat the olive oil and add fresh torn basil and 5 minced garlic cloves. Sauté until garlic is just slightly browned. Add the garlic-oil mix to the tomato sauce. On medium-low heat, cook the sauce until reduced about 1 inch from the original height. Cook longer for a thicker sauce. Constantly stir sauce so the bottom of the sauce doesn't burn.

In a separate skillet, melt the butter, and sauté the mushrooms, capers, red-pepper flakes, remaining clove of minced garlic, olives, and a pinch or two of salt. When the mushrooms are soft enough but still have a little firmness, add white wine, bring to a boil, and reduce.

To be a little daring, add a couple anchovy fillets to the skillet when sautéing the mushrooms. They will melt into the sauce and add a great flavor.

Once the wine is cooked down, combine the mushroom and tomato sauces in a skillet that is large enough for both the sauce and pasta.

Put a large pot of fresh water on the stove and bring to a boil, then add a handful of salt. Add the pasta and stir. Cook the pasta until al dente, about 10 minutes. Drain the pasta, but save 1/2 cup of the pasta water for the sauce.

Add the pasta to the sauce, along with 1/4 cup of the pasta water.

Toss everything together and add a handful of grated Parmigiano-Reggiano. Toss again.

Serve the pasta with the second handful of grated cheese and maybe a sprig of fresh basil on top.

Buon appetito!

Place all the ingredients into a 2-quart saucepot, bring to a boil, and simmer for 30 to 45 minutes. Strain.

CHUTNEY

Vanilla-wine syrup (see recipe)

2 nectarines, peaches, or apricots (or any of your favorite stone fruits), washed and diced small

³/₄ cup red onion or Vidalia onion, julienned

4 garlic cloves, peeled and thinly sliced

2 tablespoons fresh ginger, minced

1 package (2 ounces) fresh basil leaves, cut into a chiffonade

Kosher salt and freshly ground pepper

Put the syrup in a saucepot and return to a simmer. Add fruit, onion, and garlic and simmer until onions and garlic look candied (1 to 1 ¹/₂ hours). Remove from heat and stir in ginger, basil, and salt and pepper to taste. If desired, add another tablespoon of ginger. This chutney will keep in the refrigerator for a month.

FRIED POTATOES

2 pounds Yukon gold potatoes

¹/₂ pound sweet onions, julienned

¹/₄ cup duck fat, olive oil, or canola oil

1 tablespoon Italian parsley, chopped

2 tablespoons unsalted butter

1 tablespoon fresh chives, chopped

Kosher salt and freshly ground pepper

Boil whole potatoes until they're al dente. Remove from water and let cool. Peel and slice them. Melt the duck fat in a nonstick sauté pan. Add the sliced potatoes and onions. Cook until browned and onions are slightly caramelized. Finish with butter, chives, parsley, and kosher salt and pepper to taste.

Note: You can use any of the fats and oils listed; however, duck fat is very special. Leftover baked potatoes work as well as boiled Yukons.

KINILAW

BRIAN HARDESTY, ELEMENT AND
GUERILLA STREET FOOD

SERVES 4

Chef's note: This is not a ceviche. You want to serve this dish while the fish is still raw. You are basically lightly marinating everything.

1 pound of your favorite *fresh* fish (do not use frozen fish; Hardesty prefers wreckfish or striped bass.)

¹/₂ tablespoon sesame oil

1 tablespoon rice-wine vinegar

1 yellow onion, diced small

1 teaspoon ginger root, minced

2 cloves garlic, minced

1 sweet bell pepper, diced small

1 Thai chili, sliced thin

1 tablespoon cilantro, chopped

1 navel orange, segmented

¹/₂ tablespoon black sesame seeds

Sea or kosher salt

Black ground pepper

Dice the fish into ¹/₄–inch cubes and set aside at room temperature. Whisk the oil and vinegar together; reserve. Toss the onion, ginger, garlic, peppers, cilantro, orange, and sesame seeds in a bowl. Add the fish and drizzle vinegar-oil mixture over the fish mixture. Lightly toss to coat. Correct the seasoning as needed. Barely chill the mixture, about 5 minutes. Serve within 20 minutes of combining.

LAMB RAGU

VITO RACANELLI JR., MAD TOMATO

SERVES 6 TO 8

½ cup olive oil

2 cups onion, diced

½ cup carrot, diced

½ cup celery, diced

¼ cup leek, diced

1 pound ground lamb

10 fresh basil leaves

1 tablespoon garlic, chopped

1 cup red wine

2 cups mushroom stock (available at Kitchen Conservatory)

2 cups lamb stock (available at Kitchen Conservatory)

2 sprigs fresh oregano

2 sprigs fresh thyme

2 fresh bay leaves

4 cups crushed San Marzano tomatoes

1 pound cavatelli, gnocchi, or tagliatelle pasta

Pecorino cheese

Heat the oil and sweat onions, carrot, celery, and leeks. Add the ground lamb and cook until browned. Add basil and garlic. Drain off half the fat, then place the pan back over heat. Deglaze with wine.

Add mushroom stock and reduce for 2 minutes, then add lamb stock and reduce for 2 minutes more.

Tie oregano, thyme, and bay leaves together with butcher's twine and place in the pot. Add crushed tomatoes and cook for 30 to 45 minutes, or until all vegetables are soft.

Toss with cavatelli, gnocchi, or tagliatelle. Top with pecorino cheese.

MACADAMIA NUT–CRUSTED CHICKEN

ERIC KELLY, SCAPE

SERVES 4

4 6-ounce chicken breasts, boneless and skinless

Fresh black pepper

Lawry's Seasoned Salt

1 cup all-purpose flour

4 eggs, lightly beaten

1 cup panko bread crumbs, ground fine

½ cup macadamia nuts, ground fine

½ cup olive oil

24 ounces mashed potatoes (your own recipe)

8 ounces *shoyu* cream sauce (see recipe)

8 ounces papaya marmalade (see recipe)

1 tablespoon black sesame seeds

4 basil leaves, fried

Place a 2-foot piece of plastic wrap on the counter. Place the chicken breasts on the plastic, then top the chicken with another sheet of plastic. Use the flat side of a meat tenderizer to carefully pound the chicken to an even ½-inch thickness. Remove the top plastic, and season both sides of the chicken with pepper and seasoning salt.

Create a dredging station: Add flour to a pie pan. Add the eggs to a separate pie pan. Combine the ground panko bread crumbs and macadamia nuts and mix evenly. Then place the mixture into a third pie pan. Place the prepared chicken breasts in the flour and coat both sides well; shake off any excess flour. Using one hand, individually submerge the flour-coated chicken into the eggs, then place it into the panko-macadamia mixture. Coat the chicken completely on all sides.

Hold all four prepared pieces of chicken on a plate.

Heat oil in a heavy-bottomed sauté pan over moderate heat. Once it is lightly smoking, carefully place 2 pieces of chicken in the oil and cook 3 to 4 minutes on each side until breading is golden brown, taking care not to burn them. Place browned chicken on a cookie sheet. Repeat with the other two pieces. Place the chicken in a 375-degree oven for 8 to 10 minutes, until it's cooked completely through. Remove it from the oven and hold warm until ready to serve.

PAPAYA MARMALADE

    1 Hawaiian papaya, peeled, seeded, and
       diced into 1-inch pieces
    1 cup pineapple, fresh, peeled, cored, and
       diced into 1-inch pieces
    1 cup granulated sugar
    1/2 cup dry white wine

Place the papaya, pineapple, sugar, and wine in a non-reactive saucepan over moderate heat and bring to a simmer. Use a pastry brush and ice water to brush the sides of the pan and remove any crystallized sugar. Do this twice during the cooking process. Once sugar has dissolved, remove from heat and purée, using an immersion blender. Transfer to a nonreactive dish and cool in the refrigerator overnight.

SHOYU CREAM SAUCE

    2 cups heavy cream
    1/2 cup Kikkoman soy sauce

Place cream in a heavy-bottomed saucepan. Place over moderate heat and reduce by nearly half. Be careful not to let cream boil over. Once the cream is reduced, add the soy sauce. Reduce the sauce again, slightly to nappe (a consistency that lightly coats the back of a wooden spoon). A streak is left behind if you wipe your finger across the back of the spoon.

To serve: Place a scoop of mashed potatoes in the center of each serving plate.

Using a sharp knife, cut each chicken breast in half and stack two halves atop each other on top of the mashed potatoes. Place tablespoons of the papaya marmalade around the mashed potatoes at 12, 4, and 8 o'clock. Use a 2-ounce ladle to add 2 ounces of *shoyu* cream sauce over the top of the chicken.

Garnish by sprinkling a few black sesame seeds over the papaya marmalade. Finally, garnish the top of the chicken with a few stems of fried basil.

MANGO AJI

JORGE CALVO,
MANGO PERUVIAN CUISINE

SERVES 6

    4 yellow potatoes
    5 slices white bread
    3/4 cup evaporated milk
    1 large carrot
    1 stalk celery
    1 1/2 pounds chicken breast
    4 cups chicken stock
    1/4 cup vegetable oil
    2 garlic cloves, minced
    1 large onion, finely chopped
    3 tablespoon aji amarillo paste (available at
       Global Foods Market)
    1 teaspoon ground turmeric
    1/4 cup grated Parmesan cheese
    3 tablespoons walnuts, chopped
    Salt and pepper
    2 hard-boiled eggs, peeled and sliced
    10 Peruvian black olives, halved

Cook the potatoes in salted water until tender when pierced with a fork. Let cool. Peel and cut into quarters. Set aside. Place bread in a small bowl, pour evaporated milk over the bread, and soak. Set aside.

Place carrot and celery in a pot of water and bring water to a boil. Add the chicken and bring it to a simmer. Cook for 10 to 15 minutes, until chicken is cooked through. Set the chicken aside to cool. Strain broth and save 2 cups of the broth. In the same pot, sauté the garlic and onions with the aji amarillo paste and oil until onions are soft and golden. Add turmeric. Remove from the heat and let cool. Shred the cooled chicken into bite-size pieces.

In a blender or a food processor, process the evaporated milk and bread mixture and 1 $\frac{1}{2}$ cups of the reserved chicken broth. Blend until smooth.

Add the creamy bread mixture to the pot. Bring to a low simmer and stir, then add the shredded chicken. Add the Parmesan cheese. Add the walnuts and stir until hot. If necessary, thin with more chicken stock. Season it with salt and white pepper to taste.

Serve over sliced potatoes and garnish with slices of hard-boiled eggs and black olives.

MOULES-FRITES WITH HORSERADISH-SMOKED MUSSEL CREAM

JON DREJA, FRANCO

SERVES 2

- 2 pounds fresh Prince Edward Island mussels
- 2 russet potatoes
- Frying oil (high-smoke-point oil such as canola or corn oil)
- Salt and pepper
- 1 tablespoon unsalted butter
- 1 shallot, thinly sliced
- 2 tablespoons grated fresh horseradish
- 4 sprigs thyme, leaves only
- $\frac{1}{2}$ cup crème fraîche
- $\frac{1}{2}$ cup heavy cream
- 2 ounces smoked mussel butter (see recipe)
- 2 slices baguette, toasted

Clean and purge the mussels by placing them in a pot filled with lightly salted cold water for about 30 minutes before cooking. Discard any broken or open mussels. Remove mussels from the pot, brush off any remaining sand or dirt, and discard the water.

For the frites, cut the potatoes into $\frac{1}{4}$-inch batons. Place them in a bowl of ice water for at least an hour to remove the starch. Remove and blot off any excess water. Heat a pot filled halfway with frying oil to 300 degrees. Working in batches, cook the batons for 5 minutes in the oil, then drain on paper towels. Once blanched, turn the oil up to 375 degrees and fry the batons for 5 to 6 minutes, or until they are crisp and golden brown. Remove from the oil and toss with salt and pepper to taste.

For the mussels, heat a medium-size skillet and add

CONTINUED ON PG. 106

Sea Bass
With Salsa Verde

KYLE LIPETZKY, CAFÉ EAU AND EAU BISTRO

SERVES 4

3 to 5 ice cubes

1 garlic clove

1 ½ bunch parsley

1 bunch basil

½ bunch mint

1 tablespoon capers

1 teaspoon crushed red
  pepper

½ tablespoon Dijon
  mustard

1 anchovy fillet

1 ½ ounces red-wine
  vinegar

1 teaspoon black pepper

½ cup extra-virgin olive
  oil

Salt

4 sea-bass fillets

Place ice, garlic, parsley, basil, mint, capers, red pepper, mustard, anchovy, vinegar, and pepper into a blender and purée until smooth. With the machine running, add the oil and blend until the sauce is emulsified. Taste and adjust seasoning as needed.

Season and sauté sea bass until cooked through. Serve with salsa verde.

the unsalted butter. Once the butter starts to brown, add the shallot and cook until soft and translucent. Add the horseradish, thyme, and mussels to the pan and stir to make sure ingredients are evenly distributed. Add the cream and crème fraîche. Cover the pan and let the mussels cook for about 3 to 4 minutes until they all open (discard any closed ones). Turn off the heat and swirl in the smoked mussel butter. Season to taste and divide up between two bowls.

Serve the mussels with a side of frites and a slice of baguette.

SMOKED MUSSEL BUTTER

- 1/2 cup unsalted butter
- 2 ounces smoked mussels, meat only
- 1 teaspoon parsley, finely chopped
- 1 pinch salt

Mix all ingredients until the mussel meat is dissolved into the butter.

PAELLA

PEIO ARAMBURU,
BARCELONA TAPAS RESTAURANT

SERVES 6 TO 8

- 2 small chickens
- 6 cups strong chicken broth
- 1/2 teaspoon Spanish saffron
- 1/4 teaspoon smoked paprika
- 2 small onions, 1 diced
- 2 bay leaves
- 1 lemon
- 2 cups dry white wine
- 1/2 cup olive oil
- 1/2 cup Spanish chorizo
- 1/8 cup roasted red peppers, fresh or canned, diced
- 1/4 cup chopped garlic
- 1 cup canned diced tomatoes
- 18 to 24 shrimp
- 3 cups short-grain Spanish rice
- 3 teaspoons parsley, chopped
- Salt and pepper
- 1/4 cup fresh green peas
- 24 mussels
- 8 lemon wedges

Cut chicken breast into four pieces and cut the thigh into small serving sizes. Place the bones and bony part of wings and legs in a pot and cover with chicken broth. Add saffron, paprika, whole onion, bay leaves, whole lemon, and wine. Let simmer down to exactly 5 1/2 cups of broth.

Heat a 15-inch metal paella pan with oil. Add chicken and cook until golden brown. Set aside.

In the same pan, add chorizo and cook for 7 minutes.

Then add chopped onion, chopped peppers, garlic, and tomatoes. Cook until softened. Add shrimp and cook for 3 minutes. Remove the shrimp to a plate.

Add rice to vegetables-chorizo mix until well coated with the oil in the pan. Add 2/3 of the chopped parsley.

The paella can be made in advance up to this point.

Bring the broth to a boil; season with salt and pepper.

Pour the broth over the rice-vegetables-chorizo mixture, stir well, and cook uncovered for 10 minutes. Fix seasoning for the last time.

Add peas. Bury chicken, shrimp, and mussels around the pan.

Cover with aluminum foil and bake for 10 minutes at 350 degrees.

Take it out of the oven and let rest for 10 minutes.

Decorate with lemon wedges and parsley.

PAN-ROASTED MUSSELS

BOB COLOSIMO,
ELEVEN ELEVEN MISSISSIPPI

SERVES 2

2 tablespoons smoked bacon

1 teaspoon minced garlic

1/4 cup fresh tomatoes, diced

1/2 cup white wine

1/4 cup cilantro pesto (see recipe)

1 pound Prince Edward Island mussels, scrubbed

1 tablespoon mascarpone cheese

1 tablespoon unsalted butter

Salt and pepper to taste

In a heavy sauté skillet, sauté the bacon until slightly brown. Add the minced garlic and diced tomatoes and sauté for 1 minute. Add the white wine and bring to a simmer.

CILANTRO PESTO

MAKES 1 CUP

1 cup fresh cilantro tops, stems removed

1/4 cup almonds, sliced

1/2 cup Parmesan, grated

2 teaspoons garlic, minced

1/2 cup extra-virgin olive oil

1 teaspoon salt

1 teaspoon pepper

Place all ingredients in a food processor and purée until smooth. Adjust seasonings and refrigerate. Any extra pesto makes a delicious topping for grilled beef, pork, or chicken.

To serve: Add the cilantro pesto and mussels to the skillet, and let simmer for 3 to 4 minutes until the broth is reduced by half. Add the mascarpone cheese and butter. Simmer until all the mussels are open. Season to taste with salt and pepper. Serve immediately.

PAN-SEARED JUMBO SCALLOPS WITH DICED HAM IN TOMATO TRUFFLE SAUCE

JOSEPH HEMP V,
ROBUST WINE BAR

SERVES 4

8 jumbo sea scallops

1/4 cup diced prosciutto

1/4 cup diced and dried tomato (see recipe)

2 tablespoons green onions, minced

1 tablespoon parsley, chopped

1/4 cup water

2 tablespoons truffle butter (see recipe)

3 cups creamy polenta (see recipe)

DRIED TOMATOES

1 28-ounce can diced tomatoes

2 tablespoons extra-virgin olive oil

Salt and pepper

Drain the tomatoes and spread on a parchment-lined rimmed sheet pan. Toss with oil, salt, and pepper. Bake in a 400-degree oven until light brown and toasted, about 20 minutes. Stir frequently for even cooking.

TRUFFLE BUTTER

2 tablespoons garlic, minced

1/4 cup shallots, minced

1 tablespoon olive or canola oil

1/2 cup white wine

1 pound unsalted butter, cubed and at room
   temperature

1 tablespoon parsley, chopped

2 tablespoons truffle oil

Gently sweat the garlic and shallot in olive or canola oil until translucent, but do not brown. Deglaze the pan with the white wine and reduce until almost dry. Remove from heat and chill in the refrigerator until completely cold. In a stand mixer (or by hand), whip together the shallot mixture with the butter, parsley, and truffle oil. Reserve 2 tablespoons for the recipe, and the remainder can be packaged and frozen for another recipe.

POLENTA

2 cups milk

1 1/3 cups heavy cream

2/3 cup cornmeal (the finer the better)

2/3 cup grated Parmesan

Salt

Bring the milk and cream to a boil. Stir in cornmeal and reduce heat to a simmer. The polenta may seem soupy at first, but it will thicken. Stir constantly to prevent scorching. Slowly cook the polenta until all the liquid is absorbed and it has thickened, about 30 minutes. When the meal is soft and thick, stir in the Parmesan. Taste and adjust seasoning with salt.

In a *hot* large nonstick sauté pan, place the seasoned scallops. Don't fidget; let them cook and brown. When they are nicely caramelized on the first side, flip and brown the other side. Finished scallops should be mid-rare to medium. If they overcook, they will shrivel and become tough. As soon as you

flip the scallops, add the prosciutto and tomatoes. When the scallops are browned, deglaze the pan with water. Let boil and add the green onions, parsley, and truffle butter. You should end with an emulsified tomato sauce. If the sauce separates, add a tablespoon of water to make a rich ragu, not an oily mess.

To serve: Divide the polenta onto four plates. Place two scallops onto the polenta. With just the ragu in the pan, taste it. The brand of prosciutto determines the salt levels. Adjust a bit to your liking, then spoon on top of the scallops.

PAPPARDELLE ALLA BELLA NAPOLI

FRANK GABRIELE, CINI AND
IL BEL LAGO

SERVES 4

1 pound pappardelle

10 to 12 black olives, stones removed and
   coarsely chopped

2 tablespoons Italian parsley, chopped

2 tablespoons capers, drained

3 tablespoons olive oil

4 cloves of garlic, halved

4 or 5 anchovy fillets, crushed to a paste with
   a fork

2 14- to 16-ounce cans or 1 28-ounce can
   crushed tomatoes

1/2 to 1 small red chili, chopped

Salt

Fill a pasta pot with water and set the pasta to boil.
   Set aside some of the olives, parsley, and capers to use as a garnish.

In a deep pan, lightly brown the garlic in hot oil. Add anchovies.

Add the tomatoes, olives, capers, and chili. Cook over medium-high heat for 10 minutes, stirring occasionally. Add parsley and cook for a few minutes more. Cook the pasta. Drain well.

To serve: In the pan, or in a warm serving bowl, place the cooked and drained pasta, add the sauce, and mix thoroughly. Top off with a sprinkling of fresh chopped parsley if preferred.

PAPPARDELLE WITH SHORT-RIB RAGU

NY VONGSALY, BAR LES FRÈRES, BOBO NOODLE HOUSE, AND I FRATELLINI

SERVES 4

½ cup flour

Salt and pepper

¼ cup olive oil

2 tablespoons butter

4 beef short ribs

1 onion, chopped

2 carrots, peeled and chopped

1 celery stalk, chopped

2 quarts beef stock

2 cups red wine

2 bay leaves

Ragu sauce (see recipe)

Preheat oven to 375 degrees. Mix the flour, salt, and pepper in a shallow bowl. Heat the olive oil and butter in a heavy skillet. Dredge the short ribs in the flour mixture and sear in the hot skillet until brown on all sides. Transfer to a roasting pan. Add the onion, carrot, and celery to the skillet and lower the heat.

Stir until golden brown. Transfer the vegetables to the roasting pan with the short ribs. Cover with beef stock and red wine. Add the bay leaves. Cover with foil and roast for 3 hours, or until the meat is falling off the bone. Take the ribs out of the stock and let cool slightly. Strain the stock. Cover and refrigerate the stock and meat overnight or for several hours. Pull the meat from the bones and shred. Remove and discard cartilage and bone. Reserve the stock.

RAGU

3 tablespoons olive oil

3 garlic cloves, chopped

½ onion, chopped

1 can crushed tomatoes (fire-roasted if available)

Stock from short ribs

1 pound pappardelle, fresh or dry

Sea salt and pepper

Parmigiano-Reggiano, grated

Pull the short ribs and stock out of the refrigerator. Skim the fat off the stock and discard. Heat the olive oil and add garlic and onion. Cook until translucent. Stir in tomatoes and the stock. Season with salt and pepper.

Bring to a boil and reduce the heat to medium low. Add the shredded short-rib meat. Cook for 15 to 20 minutes.

Boil 3 to 4 quarts of water with a tablespoon of sea salt. Add pappardelle and cook until al dente. Strain the noodles into the sauce.

Serve with grated Parmigiano-Reggiano.

Crispy Shrimp Tacos

HELEN FLETCHER, THE ARDENT COOK AND TONY'S

SERVES 4

8 small flour tortillas

Honey-cumin coleslaw (see recipe)

Pico de gallo (see recipe)

Crispy shrimp (see recipe)

Four to 5 hours beforehand, whisk together the mayonnaise, sour cream, lime juice and zest, honey, parsley, cilantro, jalapeño pieces and liquid, cumin, and salt in a large bowl. Add the coleslaw mix and thoroughly combine the ingredients. Refrigerate the coleslaw until it's needed.

HONEY-CUMIN COLESLAW

$1/2$ cup mayonnaise

$1/2$ cup sour cream

2 tablespoons lime juice

1 tablespoon lime zest

$1 1/2$ tablespoons honey

$1 1/2$ tablespoons parsley, finely chopped

$1 1/2$ tablespoons cilantro, finely chopped

1 tablespoon jarred jalapeño peppers, finely chopped

1 tablespoon jalapeño liquid from the jar

2 teaspoons ground cumin

$3/4$ teaspoon salt

1 8 $1/2$–ounce bag shredded coleslaw mix

PICO DE GALLO

$1 1/2$ cups tomato, seeded and coarsely chopped

$1/3$ cup red onion, finely diced

1 tablespoon jarred jalapeño, finely diced

2 tablespoons cilantro, chopped

2 tablespoons lime juice

Four to 5 hours beforehand, stir together the tomato, onion, jalapeño, cilantro, and lime juice. Refrigerate the pico de gallo until it's needed.

CRISPY FRIED SHRIMP

2 egg whites

$1 1/2$ to 2 cups panko

1 pound 31- to 35-count raw shrimp, peeled and deveined

Vegetable oil

CONTINUED ON PG. 112

Place the egg white in a shallow bowl and beat it with a fork until it's foamy. Place the panko in another shallow bowl to the right. Set out a paper towel–lined baking sheet next to the panko.

Place the shrimp in the egg white, coating both sides. Put the shrimp in the panko, turning them to coat both sides in the crumbs and pressing the crumbs onto the shrimp. Remove the shrimp to the paper towel–lined baking sheet.

Preheat the oven to 200 degrees. Pour the vegetable oil into a medium-size sauté pan to a depth of ¼ inch. Heat it until it's very hot, but not smoking. The oil's temperature should be about 350 degrees. Test it by dropping a few crumbs into the hot oil; if it bubbles nicely, the oil is hot enough.

Add enough shrimp to the oil so they move freely—don't overcrowd them. The shrimp should turn a golden brown in 2 to 3 minutes on each side. Remove the shrimp with a slotted spoon and keep them warm in the oven.

To serve: Place three or four shrimp on each tortilla. Top the shrimp with coleslaw, then pico de gallo. Serve 2 tacos per person.

PARMESAN CHICKEN

JENNIFER PENSONEAU,
J.FIRES' MARKET BISTRO

SERVES 6

1 ½ cup finely ground bread crumbs

½ cup finely ground Parmesan

6 6-ounce chicken breasts, boneless and
   skinless

2 eggs, whisked

2 cups milk

Salt and pepper

Andouille-mushroom cream sauce (see
   recipe)

Preheat oven to 400 degrees. Place cutting board on a dry towel on countertop. Mix bread crumbs and Parmesan together in a bowl. Have an oven-safe dish ready to bake the chicken in. Put both chicken breasts down on the cutting board and cover with plastic wrap. Pound the chicken out so it is even thickness. It can be any size; just make sure the meat is all one thickness. Combine the eggs and milk into an egg wash. Lightly salt and pepper the meat and place it in the bread-crumb mix. Dip the meat into the egg wash, then back into crumb mix. Coat the meat with bread crumbs, pushing it in so there is a liberal amount of coating. Place in the baking pan and bake uncovered for 20 minutes, or until the internal temperature of the meat is 160 degrees. Serve with andouille-mushroom cream sauce.

ANDOUILLE-MUSHROOM CREAM SAUCE

1 tablespoon unsalted butter

6 medium-size button mushrooms, diced small

1 green bell pepper, thinly sliced

1 red bell pepper, thinly sliced

1 jalapeño, diced small

3 green onions, sliced with green part

1 link Schubert's Packing Co. andouille sausage, medium dice (or any traditional andouille with good cayenne-pepper spice)

2 cups heavy whipping cream

Heat butter in a medium saucepan. Add mushrooms and regulate heat so the mushrooms cook down and release their water. Once they are cooked, add the bell peppers, jalapeño, and green onions. Sauté until the peppers are soft, or about 10 minutes. Add the andouille sausage. Cook for another 5 minutes.

Add the cream and reduce by a quarter to half. When the sauce is thickened, season with salt to taste. Pour over Parmesan chicken and serve.

PASTRAMI-CURED SALMON WITH FLAVORS OF EVERYTHING BAGEL

NEIL ALKOBRI, BOCCI BAR

MAKES 8 4-OUNCE PORTIONS

Chef's note: For this recipe, we use grams instead of ounces because it gives us a more precise measurement, so we have the proper ratio for the cure on the salmon.

Editor's note: We added the standard measurements as well.

PASTRAMI-CURED SALMON

1/2 cup (125 grams) white sugar

3/4 cup (180 grams) brown sugar

3/4 cup (175 grams) kosher salt

2 tablespoons (28 grams) black peppercorns, toasted

2 tablespoons (28 grams) pink peppercorns, toasted

2 tablespoons (28 grams) coriander seeds, toasted

2 to 3 pounds salmon fillet

In a large mixing bowl, mix sugar, brown sugar, and salt. Spread half the mixture into the bottom of a non-reactive pan. Place the skin side down, and add the rest of the mixture onto the flesh side of the salmon. Loosely cover the fish with plastic wrap. Then weigh the fish down to help press the liquid out. Use a smaller sheet tray on top of the salmon and add a few cans from the pantry on top.

Put the whole tray in the refrigerator for 48 hours. After 48 hours, check the fish. It should feel firm to the touch. If still soft, cure for another 12 hours.

Once cured, gently rinse the cure off under cold water. In a coffee grinder, combine black peppercorns, pink peppercorns, and coriander seeds and grind until it forms a coarse mixture. Once the fish is dry, apply peppercorn-and-coriander mixture to both sides of the salmon.

In a smoker, add applewood chips. Ignite chips and bring the smoker to between 130 and 140 degrees. Once the smoker has reached the desired temperature, add salmon, skin side down, and smoke for 20 minutes.

FLAVORS OF EVERYTHING BAGEL

1 1/2 tablespoons (20 grams) garlic, julienned

2 tablespoons (30 grams) red bell pepper, cut into brunoise

1 1/2 tablespoons (20 grams) green bell pepper, cut into brunoise

1 1/4 tablespoons (18 grams) red onion, cut into brunoise

2 tablespoons (30 grams) capers

CONTINUED ON PG. 116

Bone-In Prime Rib-Eye Steak With Roasted Garlic

RACHEL OBERMEYER, PRIME 1000

SERVES 1

BONE-IN RIB-EYE STEAK

20-ounce bone-in rib-eye
  steak

Kosher salt and ground
  black pepper

1 tablespoon vegetable oil

¼ cup herb-scented beef
  fat (see chef's note)

1 head roasted garlic
  (see recipe)

ROASTED GARLIC

6 whole heads garlic

1 cup white wine

1 cup water

¼ cup vegetable oil

1 tablespoon salt

Chef's note: The 20-ounce bone-in prime beef rib-eye steak has been one of Prime 1000's signature steaks since opening. Because of the great quality and cut of beef, very little needs to be done to let the flavor of the steak come through. The secret is to brush every steak twice with herb-scented beef fat. A lot of the meat is butchered in-house. Leftover meat scraps get turned into prime burger, but the leftover beef fat is rendered down with lots of bay leaves, thyme sprigs, and rosemary sprigs. Top a juicy steak with the herb-scented beef fat and whole roasted garlic cloves and the steak will be perfect.

RIB-EYE STEAK

Preheat oven to 400 degrees. Heat a nonstick skillet over high heat. Season the steak generously with salt and pepper. Add oil to pan. When hot, hard-sear the steak on each side until very well browned. Pop in oven and cook to desired internal temperature. Remove and immediately brush with beef fat. Let the meat rest for minimum of 5 minutes. Brush again with beef fat and top with roasted garlic before serving.

ROASTED GARLIC

Preheat oven to 350 degrees. Place garlic in a casserole dish. Add equal parts water and wine until the garlic floats. Drizzle with oil and sprinkle salt over the top. Cover tightly with foil. Roast for 2 to 2 ½ hours or until very soft. Immediately remove from liquid and place in cooler to chill.

To serve: Cut off the tops of the garlic and remove the cloves. Heat a nonstick frying pan with a little vegetable oil and sear the garlic until golden brown.

1 cup (225 grams) brioche crumbs, lightly
  toasted

1 1/2 tablespoons (20 grams) white sesame
  seeds, toasted

3/4 tablespoon (10 grams) coriander seeds,
  toasted

3/4 tablespoon (12 grams) fennel seeds,
  lightly toasted

1 1/2 teaspoons (7 grams) black peppercorns,
  toasted

3/4 tablespoon (10 grams) caraway seeds,
  toasted

Preheat oven to 155 degrees. On a parchment-lined sheet tray, separate the garlic, red bell pepper, green bell pepper, red onion, and capers. Dehydrate in the oven for 2 to 3 hours, or until no moisture is present. In a coffee grinder, add brioche crumbs, sesame seeds, coriander seeds, fennel seeds, black peppercorns, caraway seeds, and dehydrated vegetables. Process until a rough mixture forms. The crumbs should be coarse enough to see individual ingredients.

LEMON AIOLI

10 cloves garlic, center stem removed

1 teaspoon salt

1 pinch black pepper

1/4 teaspoon lemon zest

1/4 cup lemon juice

6 tablespoons water

4 large egg yolks

2 teaspoons Dijon mustard

1 4/5 cup light olive oil

Bring water in a double-boiler pan to a simmer. Purée garlic, salt, pepper, lemon zest and juice, water, egg yolks, and mustard in a blender. Scrape contents of blender into the top of the double boiler and cook,

whisking constantly, until the mixture tests 150 degrees on an instant-read thermometer for 2 minutes. Remove from heat. Set mixture aside and allow to cool to room temperature. Pour oil into the garlic mixture in a slow, steady stream, while whisking constantly. Chill and use within 24 hours.

To serve: Spoon aioli in an oval on each plate. Slice salmon paper-thin and arrange on plate. Sprinkle the "flavors of everything" over the salmon and around the plate.

QUINTESSENTIAL CRAB CAKES WITH TOMATO CHUTNEY AND CHIPOTLE AIOLI

ERIC SOHN, QUINTESSENTIAL
DINING & NIGHTLIFE

SERVES 4 (2 CRAB CAKES EACH)

CRAB CAKES

1/4 cup red onion, chopped

2 tablespoons fresh cilantro, minced

1 tablespoon garlic, minced

1 tablespoon fresh parsley, minced

1/4 cup red bell pepper, minced

3/4 cup mayonnaise

1/4 cup panko crumbs

2 cans 6 1/2-ounces lump crabmeat, drained
  and squeezed dry

1/2 cup Italian dry bread crumbs

3 to 4 tablespoons vegetable oil

In a food processor fitted with steel knife blade, combine the red onion, cilantro, garlic, and parsley; pulse on and off four or five times until the mixture is well-combined but not puréed. Place the onion-garlic mixture in a medium bowl. In the same food-processor bowl, process bell pepper until it's finely minced. Drain liquid from the processed bell pepper. Add bell pepper, mayonnaise, and panko crumbs to onion-garlic mixture; stir well to combine. Add lump crabmeat; stir well to combine, and make sure that all the crabmeat is well-moistened. Divide mixture into eight equal portions; flatten gently into thick patties. Place the dry Italian bread crumbs in a shallow dish, then carefully coat both sides of the crab cakes. Place coated crab cakes on a parchment-lined sheet pan and refrigerate for at least 30 minutes before sautéing. Heat oil in large nonstick skillet over medium-high heat. Add crab cakes, in batches if necessary, and cook until golden brown on both sides, 3 to 4 minutes per side.

TOMATO CHUTNEY

- 1 cup apple cider vinegar
- ³/₄ cup nonalcoholic Reed's Ginger Brew
- ¹/₂ cup granulated sugar
- 1 28-ounce can whole tomatoes, coarsely chopped
- 1 teaspoon ground ginger

In a medium skillet, heat vinegar, ginger brew, and sugar over medium-high heat. Stir constantly to dissolve sugar; bring to a boil. Add tomatoes; reduce heat and simmer. Stir occasionally for 45 minutes to 1 hour or until most of the liquid has evaporated and mixture has thickened to consistency of (slightly loose) preserves. Stir in ground ginger. Place chutney in fine-mesh sieve set over small bowl; drain for at least 30 minutes. Discard liquid.

CHIPOTLE AIOLI
MAKES 1 CUP

- 1 cup mayonnaise
- 4 teaspoons puréed chipotle peppers in adobo sauce

In small bowl, combine mayonnaise and chipotle purée. Press mixture through a fine-mesh sieve. Keep refrigerated until ready to use.

Serve the crab cakes with tomato chutney and chipotle aioli.

RED WINE–AND–ROSEMARY BRAISED POT ROAST

DOMINIC WEISS,
BIG SKY CAFE
SERVES 4

- 5 pounds chuck roast, cut into large chunks
- Kosher salt
- Olive oil
- 2 ounces fresh rosemary, tied into 2 bundles
- 2 Granny Smith apples, peeled and diced large
- 5 carrots, peeled and diced large
- 2 large yellow onions, peeled and diced large
- ¹/₂ celery bunch, diced large
- 2 tablespoons honey
- 4 tablespoons tomato paste
- 2 cups red wine
- 2 cups red-wine vinegar
- 2 quarts beef stock
- Mashed potatoes

Heat the oven to 350 degrees.

Season the meat heavily with kosher salt and let rest a few minutes.

Heat a Dutch oven over high heat. Add a tablespoon of olive oil, just enough to coat the bottom of the Dutch oven. Sear meat in batches until browned on all sides. Remove meat and place on a pan to rest.

Add rosemary, apples, carrots, onions, and celery to the pan and cook until caramelized.

Mix in honey, tomato paste, red wine, and red-wine vinegar to deglaze the pan. Add the beef stock. Bring to a boil.

Add the meat back into the pan and place the covered pot into the oven.

Bake for 1 hour. Check meat for tenderness. Serve with your favorite mashed potatoes.

RICOTTA GNOCCHI BOLOGNESE

KYLE LIPETZKY,
CAFÉ EAU AND EAU BISTRO

GNOCCHI SERVES 4; MAKES 1 QUART
OF BOLOGNESE SAUCE

BOLOGNESE SAUCE

2 tablespoons olive oil

$^1/_2$ cup onions, diced

$^1/_2$ cup carrots, diced

$^1/_2$ cup celery, diced

2 cloves garlic, minced

8 ounces ground veal

8 ounces ground pork

4 ounces pancetta, chopped

3 tablespoons tomato paste

$^1/_3$ cup whole milk

$^1/_3$ cup white wine

$^2/_3$ cup tomato sauce

1 tablespoon fresh thyme

Chili flakes

Salt and pepper

In a large pan, heat 2 tablespoons of olive oil. Add the onions, carrots, and celery and cook until translucent. Add garlic and sweat for 2 minutes. Add veal, pork, and pancetta and cook until browned and crumbling apart. Drain fat. Add tomato paste and cook for 5 minutes. Add milk and wine and bring to boil. Add tomato sauce and return to boil, then reduce to simmer. Add thyme and cook for 45 minutes. Season to taste with chili flakes, salt, and pepper.

RICOTTA GNOCCHI

12 ounces ricotta

1 lemon, zested

1 tablespoon chive, minced

Salt

1 $^1/_4$ cups all-purpose flour, or more as needed

Fresh basil, torn into $^3/_4$-inch pieces

Combine ricotta, lemon, chives, and salt to taste in mixer with a dough hook. Mix on low, and slowly add flour until the dough comes together.

Roll into $^1/_2$-ounce balls and roll off of a fork to form gnocchi shape.

Place into a pot of boiling water and cook until dough balls float. Immediately drop into ice water to refresh, drain, and pat dry. Set aside.

Heat a nonstick sauté pan with enough oil to coat the bottom, about 2 tablespoons, and sauté the gnocchi until lightly golden brown.

To serve: Add Bolognese sauce and simmer together for one minute, or long enough to heat the sauce. Add fresh basil and serve.

RIVERBEND'S NOLA-STYLE PEEL-AND-EAT SHRIMP

SAM KOGOS,
RIVERBEND RESTAURANT & BAR

MAKES 10 HALF-POUND SERVINGS

4 quarts cold water

1 3-ounce package Zatarain's crab boil

6 tablespoons kosher or non-iodized salt

2 teaspoons ground cayenne pepper

1 large lemon, juiced and quartered

1 medium orange, juiced and quartered

1 medium lime, juiced and quartered

2 stalks celery

5 pounds raw Gulf of Mexico shrimp, in the
  shell, size 16 to 20, heads on or off, either
  white or brown

3 pounds ice cubes

Rémoulade or cocktail sauce

Pour water into a 10-quart stockpot and add Zatarain's, salt, and cayenne pepper (can add more to taste). Add the citrus juice and the cut pieces of citrus to the pot. Wash and break the celery into a few pieces. Add to water. Bring to a full rolling boil over medium-high heat. Add shrimp to the rolling boil. The shrimp will float to the top. Once shrimp are at the top, cook for 2 minutes, then turn off the heat. Immediately remove pot from hot burner. Add ice to fill the pot, but don't allow the pot to overflow. Soak the shrimp in the water with the spices and citrus for 20 to 25 minutes. Drain. Discard citrus and celery. Serve warm shrimp immediately.

Serve with rémoulade or cocktail sauce on the side.

ROAST CORNISH HEN WITH VEGETABLES

ANTHONY DEVOTI, FIVE BISTRO

SERVES 1

1 12-ounce Cornish hen or 1/2 chicken

1 to 1 1/2 teaspoons dried thyme

1 teaspoon salt

1 teaspoon pepper

1 tablespoon oil

1 cup assorted fresh vegetables, cut into
  medium chunks

Micro greens, such as pea or radish shoots

Preheat oven to 500 degrees. Rub hen with thyme, salt, and pepper. Heat oil in an ovenproof pan big enough to hold the bird, but with enough room for the vegetables. Sear the hen until the skin is golden brown. With the skin side up, place in oven for 10 minutes. Add vegetables and return to the oven for another 5 minutes.

Turn the hen so it is skin side down, stir the vegetables, and return to the oven for another 15 minutes, or until the hen is cooked through. Let rest for 5 minutes, then cut into pieces. Season pan *jus*, if needed.

On a plate, place pan *jus* and vegetables. Top with Cornish hen pieces. Garnish with micro greens.

ROASTED CHICKEN

RUSSELL PING, RUSSELL'S CAFÉ AND
RUSSELL'S ON MACKLIND

SERVES 4

3 or 4 carrots

1 large white onion

3 or 4 stalks celery

1 head garlic

Several sprigs fresh thyme

Several sprigs fresh rosemary

Several sprigs fresh sage

1/2 cup white wine

1/2 cup chicken stock

1/2 cup butter

1 chicken

Kosher salt and pepper

Ciabatta or sourdough bread

Preheat the oven to 350 degrees. Chop the carrots, onion, and celery into large chunks. Cut the garlic bulb in half. Place all the vegetables and herbs in a roasting dish. (The chef likes to use a large enamelware Dutch oven.)

Add the white wine, chicken stock, and 1/4 cup butter to the vegetables. The liquid should cover the bottom of the roasting pan, but not cover the vegetables.

Place the chicken on top of the vegetables and slather the skin with the remaining butter. Season the chicken generously with kosher salt and pepper. You want the chicken to sit high out of the pan so the hot air in the oven will brown the skin.

Roast the chicken uncovered for about 1 1/2 hours, or until the internal temperature reaches 160 degrees.

Remove the chicken from the oven and let it rest for 15 minutes before carving. Strain the drippings.

Serve this chicken over a thick slice of ciabatta or sourdough bread with some of the drippings poured over the top.

SAUTÉED QUAIL AL BRANDY

DOMINIC GALATI, DOMINIC'S

SERVES 4

8 quail

Salt and pepper

4 tablespoons butter

1/4 cup brandy

1/2 cup chopped onion

2 cloves garlic, minced

2 tablespoons flour

1 1/2 cups chicken broth

1 bunch fresh parsley

Cut each quail in half. Sprinkle lightly with salt and pepper to taste. Melt butter over high heat in sauté pan. Place quail in the butter and brown on both sides until the quail is golden brown. Add brandy and simmer for another 3 minutes.

Remove quail, set on platter, and place in a 200-degree oven to keep warm.

In the same pan that cooked the quail, add onion and garlic to the juices and cook for 2 to 3 minutes. Whisk flour into the mixture. Bring to a boil, stirring frequently. When the sauce has thickened, remove it from the heat. Season with salt and pepper. Lightly coat quail with the sauce and serve the remaining sauce separately. Garnish with parsley and serve.

SEARED WILD ALASKAN KING SALMON WITH SUCCOTASH AND SHERRY-VINEGAR GLAZE

REX HALE, BASSO, THE MARKET AT THE CHESHIRE, THE RESTAURANT AT THE CHESHIRE, THREE SIXTY

SERVES 6

36 pearl onions, roasted and peeled (see recipe)

6 4-ounce center-cut king salmon fillets

Sea salt and freshly ground black pepper

2 tablespoons olive oil

6 tablespoons unsalted butter

¾ cup thick-cut smoked bacon, chopped

1 ½ cups corn kernels, freshly shucked

18 heirloom cherry tomatoes, halved

1 ½ cup crowder peas, cleaned

2 tablespoons fresh garlic, minced

⅓ cup hard apple cider

⅓ cup heavy cream

3 ounces Parmesan cheese, grated

2 ounces micro basil

Sherry-vinegar glaze (see recipe)

Extra-virgin olive oil

Spread the onions on a sheet tray and roast at 350 degrees for 12 to 14 minutes. Cool them for 5 minutes, and while they are still warm, remove the skins by cutting one end of each onion and sliding the skin from the flesh.

Season the salmon fillets and sear over high heat in oil. Cook until the internal temperature is medium. In a separate pan, melt the butter and sauté the onions, bacon, corn, tomatoes, peas, and garlic until tender, forming the succotash.

Deglaze with cider, then add cream. Reduce and add Parmesan cheese. Season to taste with salt and pepper, and add 1 ounce micro basil.

SHERRY-VINEGAR GLAZE

1 cup sugar

1 quart balsamic vinegar

Place the sugar in a small saucepot and pour the vinegar over the top. Be sure not to get the sugar over the sides, and don't swirl the liquid. Place on medium-low heat. Reduce until it reaches the right viscosity. To determine this, drizzle a little on a plate with a spoon and set it in the refrigerator for a minute to see how it sets up. It should have the consistency of an aged balsamic vinegar.

To serve: When the fish is cooked, rest the fillets on top of the succotash. Drizzle the plate with sherry-vinegar glaze and extra-virgin olive oil and garnish with remaining micro basil.

SHRIMP AND GRITS WITH CREOLE SAUCE

AUSTIN PACKARD, COASTAL BISTRO

SERVES 5

CREOLE SAUCE

1 pound bacon, roughly chopped

1 pound smoked sausage, sliced thin on the bias

2 large green peppers, diced large

1 large yellow onion, diced large

4 ribs of celery, diced large

¼ cup Cajun spice

2 large cans diced tomatoes with juice

CONTINUED ON PG. 126

Linguini con Vongole (Linguini With Fresh Little-Neck Clams and Pancetta)

PAUL BUZZETTA, SAPORE ITALIAN CAFE

SERVES 4

4 tablespoons extra virgin
  olive oil

5 cloves fresh garlic,
  crushed

1 tablespoon pancetta,
  diced

1 cup dry white wine

1 cup clam juice

2 pounds fresh little-neck
  clams, in shells

1 tablespoon butter

Salted water

1 pound dried linguini, or
  your favorite pasta

Red-pepper flakes
  (optional)

½ cup fresh Italian
  parsley, chopped

10 basil leaves

Put 2 tablespoons of olive oil in a large saucepan. Cook garlic on medium heat. Add the pancetta and cook until browned. Add the wine, deglaze, and reduce completely.

Reduce the heat to medium/low and add the clam juice, clams, and butter. Boil uncovered and stir occasionally for about 15 to 20 minutes, or until the sauce is the desired consistency.

In a separate pot, bring salted water to a boil. Add pasta and cook for 3 minutes. Drain and mix into the pasta sauce. Raise the heat to high. Heat thoroughly, until sauce is reduced and pasta is al dente. The pasta should be coated. If desired, add red-pepper flakes.

Drizzle with remaining olive oil and garnish with chopped parsley and basil.

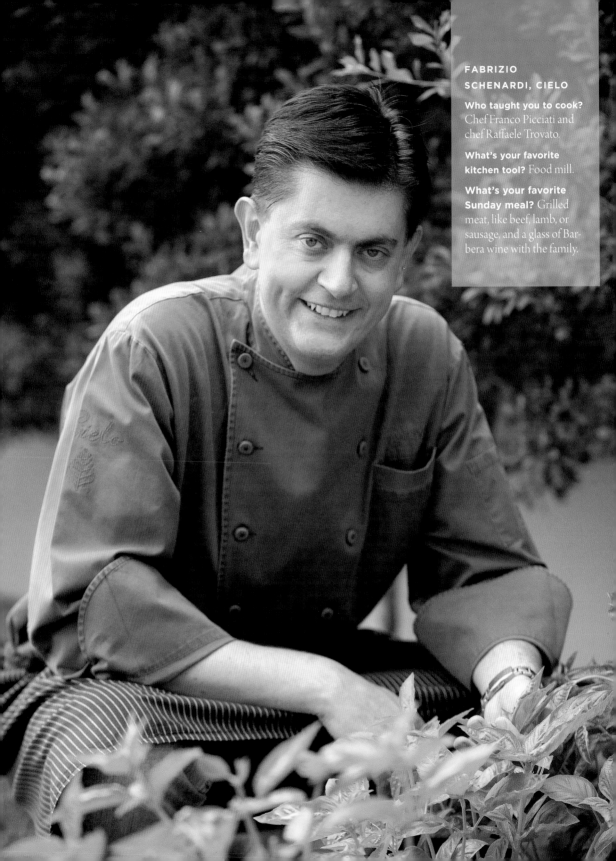

FABRIZIO SCHENARDI, CIELO

Who taught you to cook?
Chef Franco Picciati and chef Raffaele Trovato.

What's your favorite kitchen tool? Food mill.

What's your favorite Sunday meal? Grilled meat, like beef, lamb, or sausage, and a glass of Barbera wine with the family.

Duck Breast With Polenta Canederli and Marsala Sauce

FABRIZIO SCHENARDI, CIELO

SERVES 6

3 pieces of sliced shallots

2 cups apple cider

3 sticks cinnamon

3 crushed juniper berries

1/4 cup honey

6 crushed black peppercorns

6 duck breasts

Salt and pepper

CANEDERLI DI POLENTA ALLO SPECK (POLENTA DUMPLINGS WITH SPECK)

2 cups water

1 cup whole milk

10 tablespoons butter

Fine sea salt

1 1/4 cups polenta

1/4 pound speck, finely chopped

2 large egg yolks

1/4 cup Parmigiano-Reggiano or Grana Padano cheese, freshly grated

1 tablespoon flat-leaf parsley, chopped

Preheat oven to 375 degrees. Mix together the shallots, cider, cinnamon, juniper, honey, and pepper and pour over the duck. Marinate for 6 hours. Drain the duck. Heat a skillet on high until smoking. Sear the duck, skin side down, in the pan. Add salt and pepper to taste. Place in the oven and cook for 8 to 10 minutes, or until the meat is medium.

CANEDERLI DI POLENTA ALLO SPECK

In a large saucepan, combine water, milk, 3 tablespoons of the butter, and 3/4 teaspoon salt; bring it to a boil over high heat. Slowly whisk in polenta in a thin stream. Reduce heat to medium and cook, whisking constantly. Reduce heat to low and cook. For instant polenta, cook for 10 to 15 minutes, or for coarse polenta, cook for 40 to 45 minutes. Remove polenta from heat. Stir in speck, egg yolks, cheese, and parsley. Let cool for about 15 minutes, then make 40 (1-inch) dumplings.

Melt the remaining butter in a frying pan. Sauté the dumplings for about 8 minutes, or until they're golden and hot.

MARSALA SAUCE

1 tablespoon olive oil

6 tablespoons chopped shallots

1 sprig thyme

3 pears, peeled, skin reserved

1 cup dry Marsala

2 cups red-wine demi-glace

1 tablespoon olive oil–and–vegetable oil blend

Salt and pepper

CONTINUED ON PG. 126

Coat a frying pan with olive oil. Sauté shallots, thyme, and the pear skins. Deglaze it with the dry Marsala. Lower heat and reduce it by half. Add red-wine demi-glace. Simmer for 10 minutes and drain the sauce.

Dice the pear and sauté with a little bit of olive oil mixed with vegetable oil. Add salt and pepper; then, use a slotted spoon to remove the pear and add to the sauce.

COOKED VEGETABLES

    12 ounces carrots

    12 ounces parsnips

    3 ounces shallots, chopped

    2 ounces olive oil

    2 ounces butter

    Salt and pepper

    Parsley, chopped

For the vegetables, slice carrots and parsnips with a mandoline, and keep them in water. In a pan, sauté with chopped shallots, oil, and butter until soft. Add salt and pepper and chopped parsley to taste.

To serve: Put the vegetables in the middle of the plate, the duck cut in half on the top. Arrange five dumplings around the duck, and ladle the sauce on top.

Render bacon and sausage in a fry pan over medium heat. Add the peppers, onion, and celery and cook over medium heat until the onions are translucent. Mix in the Cajun spice and tomatoes. Stew it for 2 hours over low heat.

GRITS

    1 cup milk

    2 tablespoons jalapeños, seeds removed, cut into brunoise

    1/4 cup quick grits

    1 cup grated white cheddar

    Salt and pepper to taste

Bring milk and jalapeños to a boil. Reduce heat to simmer and stir in grits.

Cook until grits are thickened, then stir in the cheese. Season to taste.

FRIED ONIONS

    1 large red onion

    4 cups flour

    3 tablespoons Cajun spice

    Vegetable oil

Slice the red onion paper-thin on a mandolin. Rinse in cold water, then drain. Mix together the flour and spices and toss in the onion. Heat the vegetable oil to 350 degrees and fry the onions until golden brown. Drain.

    1 tablespoon olive oil

    1 pound 16- to 20-count shrimp, peeled and deveined

    Salt, pepper, and Cajun spice

Add olive oil to a large pan and sauté the shrimp over high heat. Season with salt, pepper, and Cajun spice to taste.

SHRIMP ALBONDIGAS

JASON TILFORD, BARRISTER'S IN CLAYTON, MILAGRO MODERN MEXICAN, MISSION TACO JOINT, TORTILLARIA MEXICAN KITCHEN

SERVES 4 TO 6

SHRIMP ALBONDIGAS

2 pounds 31- to 40-count shrimp, peeled and deveined

1 red pepper, diced fine

1 poblano pepper, diced fine

1/4 cup white onion, diced fine

2 tablespoons puréed chipotle pepper in adobo sauce

1 lime, juiced

1/2 cup cilantro, chopped

2 tablespoons sea salt

1 egg, beaten

1 cup bread crumbs (preferably panko)

Guajillo shrimp broth (see recipe)

Fresh cilantro

Lime quarters

Place shrimp in a food processor and pulse until well chopped with no large chunks remaining. Do not overprocess, or the meatballs will be gummy.

Place shrimp in a mixing bowl and fold in the peppers, onion, lime juice, chopped cilantro, and sea salt. Mix with your hands until ingredients are well incorporated. Add the egg and bread crumbs and mix again.

Form the mixture by hand into 1 to 1 1/2–ounce meatballs and place on a tray. This recipes makes about 32 albondigas.

GUAJILLO SHRIMP BROTH

6 Roma tomatoes, halved lengthwise

1 tablespoon vegetable oil

4 guajillo peppers

1/2 cup red onion, diced

1 tablespoon garlic purée

1 1/2 quarts shrimp broth or lobster broth

1 tablespoon sea salt

Preheat the oven to 450 degrees. Brush the tomatoes with half the oil and place them on a baking sheet, skin side up.

Place in the oven and roast for about 15 minutes, or until the skins brown.

While the tomatoes roast, prepare the guajillo peppers.

Place a skillet over high heat and toast the chilies for about 20 seconds on each side. Then place them in a plastic container and cover with hot water and a tight-fitting lid. Let soak for 10 minutes, then remove the peppers and rinse twice with cold water. Remove the stem and seeds and chop.

In a large saucepot, add the other half of the oil and cook the onion and garlic over medium heat until onions are translucent. Add the broth, tomatoes, peppers, and sea salt and bring to a boil. Remove from heat and let cool slightly.

Blend the broth with an immersion blender until the vegetables are chopped well and the broth is smooth. Bring back to a boil and cook the albondigas.

To serve: Bring the guajillo broth to a boil and cook the meatballs in batches, not overcrowding the pot, for 7 to 8 minutes, or until the meatballs float.

Put the meatballs in bowls. Add the broth and plenty of limes and fresh cilantro to garnish.

Tangerine Duck, Caramelized Cauliflower, Oak-Log Shiitake, Carrot Purée, and Pickled Pearl Onion

BEN LESTER, MOSAIC

SERVES 2

DUCK

2 duck breasts, skin scored

Salt and pepper

CARROT PURÉE

2 carrots, peeled and sliced

1 tablespoon butter

1 teaspoon *ras el hanout*

(Moroccan spice blend

available at Williams-

Sonoma)

½ tablespoon honey

1 pinch salt and pepper

TANGERINE GLAZE

2 tablespoons sugar

½ lemon, juiced

2 teaspoons water

1 tablespoon red-wine

vinegar

1 cup duck stock (available

at specialty stores, or

substitute chicken stock)

¼ cup tangerine juice

5 tangerine segments

Season duck with a pinch of salt and pepper, and cook over low heat, skin side down, until golden brown and crispy. Reserve the rendered fat. When ready to serve, sear the meat side for 30 seconds in reserved duck fat. Flip duck over on the skin side and place in 375-degree oven for 7 to 8 minutes, or until medium-rare. Remove from pan and allow to rest so that juices are redistributed.

Sauté carrots over a low flame with half of the butter until carrots are soft. Purée in a blender with remaining butter, *ras el hanout*, honey, salt, and pepper.

Combine sugar, lemon juice, and water in small saucepan. Caramelize the sugar over a medium flame until golden brown. Deglaze with red-wine vinegar and whisk. Add duck stock and tangerine juice. Reduce to syrupy consistency.

CARAMELIZED CAULIFLOWER

1 head cauliflower, core removed, broken into florets

3 tablespoons extra-virgin olive oil

1 teaspoon salt

½ teaspoon coarse black pepper

Toss cauliflower with olive oil, salt, and pepper. Place onto a baking pan or sheet tray in an even layer. Roast in a 450-degree oven until edges start to turn brown, approximately 3 to 5 minutes. Remove from oven and allow to cool.

CONTINUED ON PG. 130

OAK-LOG SHIITAKES

    8 shiitake caps, stems removed
    1 tablespoon extra-virgin olive oil
    1 pinch salt
    1 pinch pepper

Place shiitakes on a baking tray. Drizzle with olive oil and lightly season with a pinch of salt and pepper. Roast in a 450-degree oven, cap side down, until the gills of the shiitake are golden brown. Remove and allow to cool.

PICKLED PEARL ONIONS

    6 red pearl onions, skin removed
    Ice water
    $1/_3$ cup red-wine vinegar
    $1/_3$ cup water
    $1/_3$ cup sugar
    1 cardamom pod, crushed
    $1/_4$-inch segment cinnamon stick
    $1/_4$ teaspoon coriander seeds
    1 star anise
    $1/_4$ teaspoon black peppercorns
    1 teaspoon yellow mustard seeds

Blanch pearl onions in salted boiling water for 5 to 6 minutes, or until tender. Transfer to ice water, allow to cool, then remove to glass container. Bring the rest of the ingredients to a boil in a small saucepot. Let simmer for a few minutes to incorporate flavors and dissolve sugar. Pour the hot liquid over the onions and allow to cool. Refrigerate overnight.

To serve: While the duck is resting, place a couple spoonfuls of carrot purée on a plate. With the back of your spoon, drag the purée across to form an even layer. Lay the caramelized cauliflower, pickled onions, and rewarmed shiitakes on top of the purée.

Slice the rested duck, skin side down, $1/_4$ inch thick. Place the slices on top of the vegetables and drizzle $1/_2$ tablespoon of the glaze over the duck. Place five segments of tangerine around to garnish.

SPAGHETTI POMODORO

MICHAEL DEL PIETRO, BABBO'S, SUGO'S, TAVOLO V, AND VIA VINO

SERVES 2

2 tablespoons olive oil

1 cup fresh tomatoes, chopped

1 pinch salt and pepper

2 teaspoons garlic, minced

¼ cup vegetable stock

¼ cup tomato sauce

¼ pound spaghetti, cooked

¼ cup fresh basil, chopped

Parmigiano-Reggiano cheese, grated

In a hot skillet, heat olive oil.

Sauté tomatoes and salt and pepper for a minute. Add garlic and let the garlic cook, but not brown. Then add vegetable stock, tomato sauce, and pasta. Cook down for 3 minutes. Add basil and serve.

Garnish with fresh Parmigiano-Reggiano cheese.

STEAK WITH SYRAH SAUCE

CHRIS LEE, RIVER CITY CASINO

SERVES 8

4 rib-eye steaks

SYRAH SAUCE

2 tablespoons butter

2 tablespoons shallots, finely chopped

1 pound mushrooms, thinly sliced

¼ cup balsamic vinegar

1 cup Syrah wine

1 cup chicken stock

Melt butter in a saucepan over medium heat. Add shallots and mushrooms, then sauté for about 3 minutes. Increase heat to medium-high and add vinegar. Cook another 2 minutes. Add Syrah wine. Simmer on low for 15 minutes, or until sauce is reduced by half. Add stock. Bring to a boil, then simmer until reduced by half again.

Prepare grill and cook steaks to desired doneness. Serve with Syrah sauce.

TAGLIATELLE WITH "EGGS AND BACON"

ERIC KELLY, SCAPE

SERVES 8

1 tablespoon butter, clarified

9 bacon lardons, ¼ by ¼ by 1 inch

1 tablespoon shallot, minced

Water

1 tablespoon salt

4 ounces dry white wine

4 ounces crème fraîche

½ teaspoon grated lemon zest

1 tablespoon and ½ teaspoon kosher salt

4 ounces tagliatelle, fresh if possible

2 teaspoons Ossetra caviar

Heat butter in a sauté pan over moderate heat. Add pork lardons and sauté until edges are golden brown. Add shallot and cook until translucent, or about 1 minute.

Add salt to a large pot of water and bring to a boil. Add pasta and cook until al dente.

Meanwhile, deglaze shallots and pork with white wine and reduce by half. Stir in crème fraîche and season with lemon zest and salt.

Drain pasta and add to the pan with the sauce. Toss well to coat the pasta with the sauce.

Place the pasta on a warm serving dish. Garnish with a couple heaping teaspoons of caviar.

TUNA AND SALMON TARTARE

ELIOTT HARRIS, CHOP SHOP STL

SERVES 6

½ pound sushi-grade tuna, minced

½ pound sushi-grade salmon, minced

Guacamole (see recipe)

½ cup tartare sauce (see recipe)

30 shrimp chips, available at Asian markets

½ cup vegetable oil

TARTARE MARINADE

6 tablespoons soy sauce

3 tablespoons sake

3 tablespoons mirin (sweet rice wine)

2 tablespoons sesame oil

1 ½ tablespoons miso paste

Whisk all ingredients together until well-incorporated.

GUACAMOLE

2 avocados

1 lime, halved and juiced

1 shallot, minced

1 garlic clove, minced

½ serrano pepper, deseeded and finely chopped

3 sprigs cilantro, chopped

Sea salt

Halve and pit the avocados. Scoop out the flesh with a spoon and place in a large mixing bowl. Mash the avocados with a fork until smooth.

Add the remaining ingredients and gently fold, making sure to incorporate well.

To serve: In a small mixing bowl, combine tuna and salmon and toss with the tartare marinade.

Place a 3-inch ring mold in the center of a plate and fill it with 3 tablespoons of the guacamole. Top the guacamole with ⅓ cup of the marinated tuna and salmon and carefully remove ring mold.

In a skillet, heat the vegetable oil and fry the shrimp chips in batches until crispy. The chips can be made ahead of time, but be sure to store them in an airtight container to ensure crispiness.

Place five fried shrimp chips around each tartare.

VEGGIE TORTILLA LASAGNA

RHONDA CRANE,
MAGPIE'S RESTAURANT

SERVES 8

1 pound zucchini, sliced ¼ inch thick

1 pound yellow summer squash, sliced ¼ inch thick

4 tablespoons olive oil

2 teaspoons Cavender's Greek seasoning

3 large onions, thinly sliced

1 pound Monterey jack cheese, shredded

1 pound cheddar cheese, shredded

3 large cloves garlic, finely minced

1 ¼ teaspoons ground cumin

1 cup fresh cilantro, chopped

Nonstick baking spray

1 quart salsa, drained for 5 minutes through
  a strainer

15 6-inch corn tortillas, three cut in half

4 ears corn, cut from the cob

1 15-ounce can black beans, drained and rinsed

Preheat oven to 450 degrees. Toss zucchini and squash with 2 tablespoons of the olive oil and 1 teaspoon of the Cavender's Greek seasoning. Spread out on a baking sheet and roast on the top rack of the oven until they begin to brown, about 17 to 20 minutes.

Toss onions with remaining olive oil and Cavender's. Spread on a baking sheet and roast on the bottom rack of the oven until onions begin to brown, or about 20 to 23 minutes. Remove from the oven. Allow for it to cool enough to handle.

Reduce oven to 350 degrees.

In a medium bowl, toss together cheeses, garlic, cumin, and cilantro.

Spread about ⅓ of the salsa on the bottom of a 9- by 13-inch pan that has been sprayed with nonstick baking spray. Arrange four tortillas and two of the half tortillas over the salsa to cover the bottom of the pan. Spread half the roasted veggies, half the black beans, and half the corn over the corn tortilla layer. Top with about ⅓ of the cheese mixture. Repeat layers, ending with a top layer of tortillas, salsa, and cheese.

Bake at 350 degrees for about 45 minutes until bubbly and heated through.

Allow the lasagna to cool and set before cutting.

Sides

ASPARAGUS WITH CITRUS BEURRE BLANC

ERIC SOHN AND BRYAN SMITH,
QUINTESSENTIAL DINING & NIGHTLIFE

SERVES 20 TO 25 PEOPLE

Water

Salt

Ice cubes

2 pounds asparagus

2 tablespoons canola oil

2 teaspoons garlic, minced

Kosher salt

Fresh-cracked black pepper

Citrus beurre blanc (see recipe)

Bring a large pot of water to a boil. Add salt for flavor.

Prepare an ice bath.

Trim the bottom ends of the asparagus. Add the asparagus to the boiling water for 45 to 90 seconds, depending on the thickness of the pieces.

Remove the asparagus from the boiling water and place it in the ice bath to blanch it. Blanching helps the asparagus cook more evenly on the grill.

Remove the asparagus from the ice water after 5 minutes. (Leaving the asparagus in the ice bath for more than 10 minutes will make it soggy.)

Toss the asparagus with a few tablespoons of canola oil and the fresh minced garlic, and season it with kosher salt and fresh-cracked black pepper to taste. (Use canola oil instead of olive oil because it has a higher smoke point.)

Place the asparagus on the grill and cook it for a few minutes, until it is grilled to your liking.

CITRUS BEURRE BLANC

1 cup white-wine vinegar

2 lemons, juiced

1 cup orange juice

2 bay leaves

1 small bunch parsley stems

2 fresh thyme stems

2 shallots, sliced thin

15 black peppercorns

1/4 cup heavy whipping cream

1 pound butter, cold, cut into small pieces

1 cup white wine (chardonnay or sauvignon blanc)

Kosher salt

Place all of the ingredients except the whipping cream and kosher salt in a large pot. Bring the liquid to a boil, and cook it until the mixture has reduced to 10 percent of its original volume.

Add the heavy cream and cook the liquid for 2 minutes. Over low heat, whisk the butter into the mixture and stir until it's melted.

Taste and add kosher salt to achieve the desired flavor. Strain the sauce through a fine chinois.

Note: Like a hollandaise, this sauce will break if it is left at room temperature or heated too much. One trick is to use a thermos for sauces—just be sure to never use the thermos for coffee, because it will pick up the flavor. You can hold beurre blanc, hollandaise, and other emulsified sauces in the thermos for a long period of time, and the sauce won't break.

BUTTERNUT SQUASH–AND–FENNEL CAPONATA

KYLE LIPETZKY,
CAFE EAU AND EAU BISTRO

SERVES 6

2 tablespoons fat/cooking oil

2 large butternut squash, peeled, diced medium

1 ½ cups Brussels sprouts, halved

2 large fennel bulb, diced medium

½ cup red onion, diced small

½ cup celery, diced small

2 white anchovies

½ teaspoon chili flakes

½ cup red pepper, diced small

1 jalapeño, diced small

¼ cup dried cranberries

¼ cup capers, drained

½ cup honey

½ cup red-wine vinegar

¼ cup pine nuts, toasted

Salt and pepper

Add the oil to a sauté pan. Pan-roast the butternut squash, Brussels sprouts, and fennel until it is lightly caramelized. The vegetables should be al dente. Set them aside.

In the same sauté pan, sweat the onion and celery for 2 minutes. Add the anchovies and sauté them until they have broken down. Add the chili flakes and toast them for 1 minute. Add the red pepper, jalapeño, cranberries, and capers, and sauté it all for 3 minutes..

Deglaze the pan with the honey and red-wine vinegar. Reduce the mixture by half. Return the butternut squash, Brussels sprouts, and fennel to the pan, add the pine nuts, and cook the dish for 2 minutes. Salt and pepper to taste.

CAULIFLOWER-AND-TRUFFLE RISOTTO

VITO RACANELLI, MAD TOMATO

SERVES 6 TO 8

2 cups onion, chopped

1 tablespoon garlic, chopped

4 tablespoons olive oil

3 cups cauliflower, chopped

1 quart plus 3 cups chicken stock

¼ cup heavy cream

1 cup arborio rice

½ cup white wine

¼ cup mascarpone

1 cup grated Parmesan cheese

1 tablespoon unsalted butter

2 tablespoons white-truffle oil

Salt and pepper

Cook 1 cup of the onion and the garlic in 2 tablespoons of the olive oil until they're translucent.

Add the cauliflower and 3 cups of the chicken stock. Cook this until the vegetables are completely soft. Add the cream and reduce the liquid for 3 to 5 minutes. Purée the mixture in a blender until it's smooth and creamy.

In a heavy-bottomed pot, sauté the remaining cup of the onions in the remaining 2 tablespoons of olive oil. Add the rice and deglaze the pot with the wine.

In a separate pot, bring the remaining quart of the chicken stock to a simmer. Slowly add the chicken stock to the rice until the rice is cooked, about 20 minutes. When the rice is cooked, mix in the cauliflower purée, mascarpone, Parmesan, butter, and truffle oil. Add salt and pepper to taste.

ERIC HEATH AND JENNY CLEVELAND, CLEVELAND-HEATH

What is one must-have ingredient? Eric: Garlic. **Jenny:** Three Crabs fish sauce.

What is your favorite comfort food? Eric: Anything in sandwich form. **Jenny:** My mom's cherry pie.

What's your favorite cooking tool? Eric: MAC knife. **Jenny:** Cake tester.

Brussels Sprouts

ERIC HEATH AND JENNY CLEVELAND, CLEVELAND-HEATH

SERVES 8

3 tablespoons olive oil

5 cups Brussels sprouts,
quartered

3 tablespoons capers

Salt

Lemon juice

⅓ cup Parmesan cheese,
grated

Preheat the oven to 450 degrees. Heat a large oven-safe sauté pan on the stove until it is very hot. Add a small amount of olive oil and heat it just shy of its smoking point. Add the Brussels sprouts cut side–down and reduce the heat to medium. Caramelize the cut sides of the Brussels sprouts. Once dark brown caramelization forms on the cut sides, toss the Brussels sprouts in the pan to allow the other sides to caramelize as well. Place the pan in the oven and cook the Brussels sprouts until they're tender, about 5 to 10 minutes.

Remove the Brussels sprouts from the oven, place them in a mixing bowl, and add the capers. Season them with salt, a squeeze of lemon, and the remaining olive oil, then sprinkle them with the Parmesan before serving.

ECLIPSE POTATO AND SMOKED GOUDA GRATIN

ISSAC HARDWRICT, ECLIPSE

SERVES 12

1 stick butter, melted

1/2 cup all-purpose flour

2 cups heavy cream

2 large eggs

1/2 cup plain bread crumbs

1/2 teaspoon oregano

1/2 teaspoon thyme

1/2 teaspoon kosher salt

Nonstick baking spray

4 to 5 pounds Yukon Gold potatoes, skin on, sliced 1/8 inch thick with a mandoline

1 pound smoked Gouda, sliced 1/8 inch thick

Granulated garlic

Kosher salt

Freshly ground black pepper

In a small pot, melt the butter and mix it with the flour until smooth and golden brown. In a medium saucepan, bring the cream just to a boil, but do not let it boil. Slowly drizzle the hot butter-flour mixture into the hot cream, whisking quickly to incorporate. Cook for a minute or two, whisking continuously. Remove from heat. When slightly cool, vigorously whisk in the eggs one at a time, until the mixture is smooth and spreadable. Set aside about 2/3 cup sauce for the top.

In a small bowl, combine the bread crumbs with the oregano, thyme, and kosher salt.

Heat the oven to 350 degrees. Line the bottom and sides of a 9- by 12- by 4-inch baking dish with parchment paper. Spray with nonstick baking spray.

Assemble gratin. For the first layer, shingle a single layer of potatoes crosswise across the pan, overlapping the potatoes by half. Sprinkle with garlic, salt, and pepper. Spread 1/4 of the sauce over the top. For the second layer, shingle another layer of potatoes, lengthwise. Sprinkle with seasonings and spread another 1/4 of the sauce. For the third layer, arrange Gouda slices, covering the potatoes without overlapping the cheese. Repeat the first and third layers. Repeat the second layer, using small potato pieces at the edges to build a level surface. For the final layer, arrange large, perfectly shaped potato slices; sprinkle with seasoning. Spread reserved sauce over the top.

Spread seasoned bread crumbs over the top, pressing with your hands to smooth and pack the crumbs. Cover the top with parchment paper, tucking the sides into the bottom parchment layer to create a sort of parchment oven. Insert a second 9- by 12- by 4-inch pan inside to gently compress the gratin.

Bake for 50 minutes. Uncover and bake for 10 minutes more. Let cool. Then refrigerate for several hours until firm. Invert the parchment onto a counter and cut the gratin into 12 pieces.

Chef's note: At Eclipse, this dish is served by sautéing each piece in a hot, oiled skillet. Turn once to brown both the bottom and top. Then serve the gratin with a grilled strip steak, roasted green beans, and a flavored butter.

EGGPLANT INVOLTINI WITH FONTINA CHEESE, SPINACH, AND CAPELLINI NOODLES

JOHN MINEO,
JOHN MINEO'S ITALIAN RESTAURANT

SERVES 4

- 1 1-pound eggplant
- 1/4 to 1/2 cup extra-virgin olive oil
- 1/4 teaspoon salt
- 1/2 pound capellini noodles
- 4 cups marinara sauce
- 1 bunch fresh spinach, steamed and chopped
- 1 cup fontina cheese, shredded
- 1/2 cup Romano cheese, shredded
- 1/2 cup Parmigiano cheese, shredded
- 1/4 teaspoon ground black pepper
- Fresh parsley or basil, minced (optional)

Preheat the oven to 400 degrees. Slice the eggplant lengthwise into 12 quarter-inch-thick slices. Lightly brush each side with olive oil and sprinkle the slices with the salt.

Arrange the slices on one or two baking sheets and bake them for about 30 minutes, until the eggplant is golden brown in spots, switching the positions of the baking sheets halfway through the cooking time.

Remove the eggplant from the oven and let it cool slightly, then stack the slices together to trap moisture and ensure that they are soft enough for rolling. (This can be made ahead and stored in a sealed container in the refrigerator for up to three days.)

Boil the capellini noodles, then drain them and transfer them to a large bowl. Working quickly to avoid clumping, mix the noodles with 1 cup of the marinara sauce to thoroughly coat each strand of pasta.

Combine the capellini, spinach, half of the fontina cheese, half of the Romano cheese, and half of the Parmigiano cheese. Season well.

Spread 1 1/2 cups of the marinara sauce in a large baking dish, then prepare the involtini. Place a generous amount of the stuffing mixture on the narrow end of an eggplant slice and roll it snugly. Place the roll seam side–down in the baking dish. Repeat this with the remaining stuffing and eggplant slices. Spread the remaining 1 1/2 cups of marinara sauce on top.

Sprinkle the remaining fontina, Parmigiano, and Romano cheeses over the top of the involtini. (This can be made ahead. If so, cover the baking dish tightly with plastic wrap and refrigerate it up to 2 days.)

Preheat the oven to 350 degrees. Bake the involtini for 10 minutes, until they're heated through. Sprinkle the finished involtini with minced fresh parsley or basil to add color.

HAWAIIAN-STYLE FRIED RICE

JUSTIN HAIFLEY,
THE SHACK PUBGRUB AND
THE TAVERN KITCHEN & BAR

SERVES 6 TO 8

1 pound bacon, diced

1 cup Portuguese-style sausage (available at Global Foods Market), diced large

2 tablespoons *rayu* (Japanese sesame chili oil)

4 cups cooked white rice

1/4 cup carrots, diced small

1/4 cup onion, diced small

3 tablespoons *shoyu* (soy sauce)

3 tablespoons oyster sauce

4 eggs, whisked

1/4 cup green onion, diced

1/4 cup peas

Fresh-cracked black pepper

In a wok over high heat, cook the bacon and sausage until the fat has rendered. Add the sesame chili oil, then the rice, and cook them until the rice is "toasted." Add the carrots and onion and cook until they're tender. Stir in the soy sauce and oyster sauce until the rice is coated.

Make a well in the middle of the wok by pushing the rice up the sides, and pour the eggs in the middle. Add the green onion, the peas, and black pepper to taste. Scramble the eggs and mix them in until all of the ingredients have been evenly distributed. Serve the dish immediately.

MUSHROOM RISOTTO

ERIC SOHN, QUINTESSENTIAL
DINING & NIGHTLIFE

SERVES 8

6 1/2 cups chicken stock

5 tablespoons butter

1/2 cup onion, diced

1 cup shiitake mushrooms, diced

1 cup crimini mushrooms, diced

2 tablespoons shallots, minced

3 cloves garlic, minced

2 cups arborio rice

1/3 cup dry white wine or dry vermouth

2 tablespoons heavy whipping cream

1 tablespoon fresh thyme leaves, minced

1/4 teaspoon salt

1/4 teaspoon ground white pepper

1/2 cup Parmesan cheese, grated

In a medium saucepan, heat the stock over medium heat and keep it warm, but do not boil it. In a large saucepan, melt the butter over medium-high heat. Add the onion and cook, stirring often, until it wilts, 1 to 2 minutes. Stir in the mushrooms, shallots, and garlic and cook them until the mushrooms soften, 2 to 3 minutes.

Add the rice and cook it, stirring constantly, for 2 minutes. Add the wine (or dry vermouth) and 1/2 cup of the heated stock, and stir often until the liquid is absorbed. Add the remaining stock, 1/2 cup at a time, stirring frequently until the liquid is absorbed before adding additional stock, about 20 minutes. When the rice is tender and very creamy, stir in the cream, thyme, salt, and white pepper. Stir in the Parmesan and serve the dish immediately.

NANNA'S STUFFED MELANZANE

RICH LoRUSSO,
LoRUSSO'S CUCINA

SERVES 4

2 eggplants, tops trimmed off, sliced
    lengthwise into 1/4-inch slices

2 tablespoons olive oil, plus more for the
    eggplant, or nonstick baking spray

1/2 cup onion, minced

1 tablespoon garlic, minced

1 tablespoon fresh basil

1 teaspoon fresh black pepper

1/2 cup vino rosso

1 28-ounce can whole peeled San Marzano
    tomatoes, hand-crushed

2 tablespoons tomato paste

1/4 cup parsley, chopped

2 teaspoons sea salt

1 pound ground chuck

1 pound ground veal

1/3 cup red onion, minced

1/3 cup Parmesan cheese

1/3 cup Italian bread crumbs

1/2 teaspoon salt

1/4 teaspoon pepper

2 tablespoons whole milk

2 eggs

2 tablespoons parsley, minced

1/2 pound fontina cheese, cubed

1 large yellow peppers, deseeded and cut
    into strips

Spinach or greens, sautéed

1 handful Parmesan cheese, grated

Preheat the oven to 325 degrees. Submerge the eggplant slices in salted cold water for 20 minutes. (This can be done in advance.) Drain the slices and spray them with olive oil or cooking spray. Bake the slices for 10 minutes to soften them. Set the eggplant slices aside to cool.

To prepare the sauce, heat the olive oil in a pan and sauté the onion and garlic until golden. Add the basil, black pepper, wine, tomatoes, tomato paste, chopped parsley, and sea salt. Cook the sauce for 20 minutes over medium-low heat.

To make the stuffing, mix the ground chuck, ground veal, onion, Parmesan, bread crumbs, 1/2 teaspoon salt, and 1/4 teaspoon pepper with the whole milk, eggs, and minced parsley.

Pour half of the sauce into a baking dish. Form an egg-size portion of stuffing, top it with a nickel-size piece of fontina cheese in the center, and place it on a slice of the cooked eggplant. Roll up the slice of eggplant and place it seam side–down in the baking dish. Continue this process with the rest of the eggplant and stuffing. Cover the rolled eggplant slices with the remaining sauce, and top each roll with a yellow-pepper strip.

Cover the baking dish and bake it at 325 degrees for 45 minutes, then remove the cover and bake it for an additional 10 minutes. Let the dish rest for 15 minutes. Serve the eggplant with sautéed spinach or greens of your choice, and top it with grated Parmesan cheese.

JASON TILFORD, BARRISTER'S IN CLAYTON, MILAGRO MODERN MEXICAN, MISSION TACO JOINT, TORTILLARIA MEXICAN KITCHEN

What is your favorite cookbook? *Mexican Cooking* by Diana Kennedy.

Name your favorite restaurants (aside from your own). Pastaria, Mai Lee, and The Libertine are three that are killing it right now.

What's your favorite kitchen tool? A 12-inch Global chef's knife.

Mango Salsa

JASON TILFORD, BARRISTER'S IN CLAYTON, MILAGRO MODERN MEXICAN, MISSION TACO JOINT, AND TORTILLARIA MEXICAN KITCHEN

SERVES 4 TO 6

2 ripe fresh mangoes

1 habanero chili

$1/4$ cup red pepper, finely diced

$1/4$ cup green onion, chopped

1 lime, juiced

1 tablespoon sea salt

$1/4$ cup fresh cilantro, chopped

Prepare the mango by peeling and dicing into $1/4$–inch pieces. Remove the seeds and membranes from the habanero and finely mince, almost to a purée. Place the mango, red pepper, green onion, lime juice, salt, and cilantro in a mixing bowl and mix until well-combined. Start by adding half the habanero and check the heat level before adding the other half. If the habanero is too spicy, substitute a jalapeño or serrano chili.

RED-WINE RISOTTO WITH MUSHROOMS AND PEAS

LISA SLAY, REMY'S KITCHEN & WINE BAR

SERVES 6

¼ cup olive oil

½ cup onion, chopped

2 cups mushrooms (your choice), sliced

1 ½ tablespoons garlic, peeled and chopped

1 teaspoon kosher salt, plus more

½ teaspoon black pepper

2 cups (1 pound) arborio rice

2 cups red wine

4 cups vegetable broth

1 cup peas, fresh or frozen

8 ounces pecorino cheese, shredded

Heat the oil in a large heavy saucepan over medium heat. Add the onion, mushrooms, garlic, salt, and pepper. Cook the vegetables until they're almost tender, 2 to 3 minutes. Add the rice and stir for 1 minute. Add the wine and simmer, stirring constantly, until it is completely absorbed, 1 to 2 minutes.

Add ½ cup of the vegetable broth and stir until it is almost absorbed, 1 to 2 minutes. Continue cooking the rice, adding the broth ½ cup at a time, stirring constantly and allowing each addition to absorb before adding the next.

Cook the risotto for 20 to 25 minutes, until the rice is tender but still firm and the mixture is creamy, adding additional warm broth by the ¼ cup if the risotto is dry.

Mix in the peas and half of the pecorino. Remove the risotto from the heat. Add more salt to taste. Divide the dish among six shallow bowls. Sprinkle the risotto with the remaining pecorino.

ROASTED BRUSSELS SPROUTS WITH PANCETTA

JIM FIALA, ACERO AND THE CROSSING

SERVES 10

3 pounds Brussels sprouts

7 ounces pancetta, diced small

3 tablespoons unsalted butter

Salt

Extra-virgin olive oil

This dish can be served as a small side or tossed with orecchiette pasta and Parmesan cheese.

Preheat the oven to 400 degrees. Cut the bases off the Brussels sprouts and remove the outer leaves. Cut the sprouts into quarters.

Heat a heavy-bottomed skillet over medium heat. Add the pancetta and cook until lightly browned. Add the sprouts, butter, and salt. Sauté until the sprouts begin to brown, about 2 minutes.

Place the skillet in the oven and bake for 7 minutes, or until the sprouts are brown on the outside and soft inside.

Transfer to a warm serving bowl and top with a drizzle of extra-virgin olive oil.

ROASTED BUTTERNUT SQUASH WITH CHICKPEAS AND CUMIN

CHRIS LEE, RIVER CITY CASINO

SERVES 8

1 small butternut squash

2 tablespoons olive oil

4 scallions, sliced into thin diagonal strips

1 fresh red chili pepper, sliced into thin rings

1/4 cup cooked chickpeas

1 tablespoon cumin seeds

1/2 cup vegetable stock

Salt and pepper

1 small bunch cilantro

Preheat the oven to 350 degrees. Peel the squash, cut it in half, and scoop out the seeds. Cut the squash into 2-inch cubes, and toss the cubes in the olive oil. Place the squash in a shallow roasting pan and roast it until it starts to brown around the edges.

Combine the scallions, chili pepper, chickpeas, cumin seeds, and stock in a small pot and bring the mixture to a boil. Pour this seasoned stock over the squash and roast it in the oven for another 10 minutes. Season the squash with salt and pepper and garnish it with cilantro.

ROASTED CORN–AND–RED PEPPER MEDLEY

ROBERTO TREVINO, AMIGOS CANTINA AND LA CANTINA

SERVES 4

4 ears fresh corn, grilled and sliced off the cob

1 red bell pepper, diced small

1 or 2 pickled jalapeños, seeded and diced small

1/4 cup fresh cilantro, chopped

2 garlic cloves, peeled and minced

1/4 cup green onion, sliced

Kosher salt

Black pepper

1 lemon, juiced

2 teaspoons olive oil, plus more as needed

Combine the grilled corn with the red bell pepper, jalapeños, cilantro, garlic, and green onion, and season the mixture well with the kosher salt and pepper. Toss the vegetables with the lemon juice and olive oil, using more olive oil, if necessary, to bind the mixture together.

Truffled Twice-Stuffed Potato

BRANDON BENACK, TRUFFLES
SERVES 2

Kosher salt

1 large Idaho potato

**¼ pound applewood-
smoked bacon**

**1 bunch green onions,
thinly sliced**

1/4 cup sour cream

**1 cup white cheddar
cheese, grated**

**1 tablespoon white-
truffle oil**

Fresh-cracked pepper

Preheat the oven to 350 degrees. Line a baking pan with kosher salt. Wash and dry the potato and place it on top of the salt. Bake the potato until it is cooked, about 30 to 45 minutes. Let the potato cool, then slice it in half lengthwise. Scoop out the inside of the potato and reserve the shell.

Dice the bacon and render it in a skillet until it is crispy. Reserve the bacon fat. Combine the potato filling with the bacon, green onions, sour cream, ½ cup of the cheese, and truffle oil. Add the reserved bacon fat to taste. Once combined, season the mixture to taste with kosher salt and fresh-cracked black pepper.

Add the potato mixture back into potato shell, and do not be afraid to overstuff it. Top the potato with the remaining ½ cup of cheese and bake it in a 350-degree oven for 8 to 10 minutes.

ROASTED MUSHROOMS

DANA HOLLAND,
JILLY'S CUPCAKE BAR & CAFÉ

SERVES 10 TO 12

Dana Holland loves all roasted mushrooms and changes the ingredients in this dish based on what he has in the refrigerator and pantry. For a less expensive version, stick with white and crimini mushrooms. For a more elaborate version for special occasions, add oyster mushrooms, shiitakes, chanterelles, morels, or any other fresh mushrooms.

- 2 pounds assorted mushrooms
- 1/4 cup olive oil
- 12 cloves garlic, peeled and sliced
- 1/4 cup sherry or white wine
- 1/4 cup sherry vinegar
- 1 tablespoon paprika
- 1 tablespoon fresh rosemary, chopped
- 1/2 teaspoon red-pepper flakes
- 1/2 tablespoon kosher salt or sea salt
- Ciabatta bread, grilled, or fresh goat-cheese log (optional)

Preheat the oven to 425 degrees.

Clean the mushrooms of any dirt.

If you are using white or crimini mushrooms, lightly rinse the mushrooms with water.

Cut the mushrooms into slices a bit larger than the size of a quarter; the mushrooms will shrink while cooking.

Place the mushrooms in a bowl and toss them with the olive oil, garlic, sherry or white wine, vinegar, paprika, rosemary, red-pepper flakes, and salt.

Spread the mushrooms onto a rimmed cookie sheet or in a large casserole dish so they are not more than two deep. If the pan is too small, the mushrooms will not cook evenly, and if it is too large, they might burn.

Bake the mushrooms for 15 minutes.

Toss the mushrooms, then cook them for another 10 minutes.

Check the mushrooms; the liquid should be reduced to a lightly thickened glaze.

When the mushrooms are done, taste them again, add salt as desired, and allow them to cool.

Serve these mushrooms warm or at room temperature.

Note: Holland likes to splash the mushrooms with sherry and additional olive oil prior to serving them with thick slabs of grilled ciabatta bread slathered in olive oil.

The mushrooms are also good chopped and served over a log of fresh goat cheese.

SAVORY BUTTERNUT-SQUASH SOUFFLÉ WITH APPLE CHUTNEY

GREG ZIEGENFUSS,
BUTLER'S PANTRY

SERVES 6

Note: This soufflé is excellent with julienned Black Forest ham or roast pork—or as a perfect vegetarian first course.

- 1 small yellow squash, diced medium
- 1 small acorn squash, peeled and finely chopped
- 1/2 small yellow onion, diced fine
- 1/2 cup butter
- 1 tablespoon garlic, peeled and minced
- 1 cup all-purpose flour

2 teaspoons salt

1 teaspoon white pepper

1/2 cup whole milk

6 large eggs, separated

1/2 cup grated Gruyère cheese

Salt

Cream of tartar

Butter

Apple chutney (see recipe)

Black Forest ham or roast pork, julienned
(optional)

In a heavy-bottomed saucepot, sauté the yellow squash, acorn squash, and onion in the butter until they're softened.

Add the garlic and sauté it until it's aromatic. Add the flour, salt, and white pepper, stirring with a wooden spoon over medium heat for approximately 5 minutes.

With a balloon whisk, combine the whole milk and egg yolks. Stir this into the squash mixture and cook it until it's thickened. Mix it thoroughly, and be sure to scrape the sides of the pot.

Remove the pot from the heat and stir in the Gruyère cheese. Allow this mixture to cool for an hour.

Meanwhile, whip the egg whites with a pinch of salt and a pinch of cream of tartar until firm peaks form. Fold the whipped egg whites into the cooled squash mixture.

Preheat the oven to 325 degrees.

Butter soufflé molds 2 inches deep by 3 inches in diameter.

Scoop or pipe the mixture into the molds and bake it for approximately 30 minutes in a standard oven or 20 minutes in a convection oven.

Unmold and serve it immediately with the apple chutney and optional ham or roast pork.

APPLE CHUTNEY

1 cup apple-cider vinegar

1 cup local honey

2 tablespoons fresh ginger root, minced

2 tablespoons garlic, peeled and minced

2 teaspoons cinnamon

2 teaspoons salt

1 teaspoon white pepper

1 pound local Granny Smith apples, cored,
diced medium

1 lemon, juiced and zested

1/2 cup golden raisins

1/2 cup dried cranberries

Bring the vinegar and honey to a boil in a medium heavy-bottomed non-aluminum saucepot.

Lower the heat and add the ginger, garlic, cinnamon, salt, and white pepper.

Reduce the mixture by half.

Toss the apple pieces with the lemon juice and zest. Add the apple-lemon mixture, raisins, and cranberries to the saucepot and cook them until the apples are softened and the chutney thickens.

Note: This apple chutney can be refrigerated for up to two weeks. In addition to nicely accompanying pork, it is good with potato pancakes.

SMOKED CORNBREAD

MIKE EMERSON,
PAPPY'S SMOKEHOUSE

SERVES 8 TO 10

SMOKED CORN

    Apple and cherry wood chips

    Cold water

    2 or 3 ears corn, shucked

Soak the wood chips in a large bowl of cold water for at least 30 minutes. Drain the chips and scatter them in the bottom of a stove-top smoker (or your smoker of choice). Heat the chips over medium-low heat until they are smoky, about 10 minutes.

   Place the shucked corn on the rack of the smoker. Smoke the corn for about 20 minutes. Set the corn aside to cool.

   When it is cool, cut the corn from the cob.

CORNBREAD

    3 tablespoons butter

    3 tablespoons canola oil

    1 1/2 cups flour

    2/3 cup brown sugar

    1/2 cup cornmeal

    1 teaspoon salt

    1 tablespoon baking powder

    1 1/4 cups buttermilk

    2 large eggs

    1/3 cup canola oil

    4 tablespoons butter, melted

    2 jalapeños, diced

    2 to 3 ears smoked corn (see recipe)

Preheat the oven to 350 degrees. Grease a 9- by 13-inch baking dish with 3 tablespoons of butter and

3 tablespoons of canola oil, and preheat the dish in the oven. In a large bowl, mix the flour, brown sugar, cornmeal, salt, and baking powder. In a separate bowl, whisk the buttermilk, eggs, oil, and melted butter until they're well-blended. Add the wet ingredients to the dry ingredients, and mix them well to combine. Fold in the jalapeños and smoked corn. Pour the batter into the preheated baking dish. Bake the cornbread for 20 minutes, or until it's golden brown and an inserted toothpick comes out dry. Serve it hot.

SPINACH-ARTICHOKE CASSEROLE

VITO RACANELLI, MAD TOMATO

SERVES 6 TO 8

    1/2 cup onion, diced

    1 tablespoon garlic, chopped

    2 tablespoons olive oil

    1 pound spinach, blanched and drained

    8 ounces artichoke hearts or baby artichokes,
        cleaned and cooked

    1 cup heavy cream

    1/4 cup mascarpone

    1/2 cup Parmesan cheese, grated

    1/4 cup lemon juice

    Salt and pepper

    3/4 cup plain bread crumbs

    1/8 cup basil, chopped

    1/4 cup Parmesan cheese, grated

    1 teaspoon lemon zest, chopped

    1/4 cup olive oil

Preheat the oven to 350 degrees. Sauté the onion and garlic in olive oil over medium heat until they are soft and translucent. Add the spinach and artichokes. Sauté the ingredients until they're mixed well. Add the cream, and reduce the mixture for 3 to 5 minutes.

Add the mascarpone, $\frac{1}{2}$ cup Parmesan, and lemon juice, and season the mix with salt and pepper to taste. Spread the mixture in a casserole dish. Mix the bread crumbs, basil, $\frac{1}{4}$ cup Parmesan, lemon zest, and olive oil with salt and pepper to taste, and sprinkle this topping over the casserole. Bake the casserole for 15 to 20 minutes, or until the top has browned.

SWEET-AND-SOUR GREEN BEANS

TONY ALMOND, ALMONDS RESTAURANT

SERVES 4

2 14 $\frac{1}{2}$-ounce cans French-cut green beans

6 slices bacon

$\frac{1}{3}$ cup sugar

$\frac{1}{2}$ cup vinegar

1 medium onion, diced

Salt and pepper

Rinse the green beans in cold water. (Canned beans work better for this recipe than fresh ones.)

Drain the green beans and set them aside. In a pan, fry the bacon until it is crisp. Save the drippings.

Drain the bacon, crumble it, and set it aside. Stir the sugar and vinegar into the bacon drippings. Add the green beans, the onion, and salt and pepper to taste.

Cover and simmer the green beans over low heat. (The longer they cook, the better they taste.)

Top the green beans with crumbled bacon before serving.

Desserts

BACON-CHOCOLATE RICE KRISPIES TREATS

DAVID TIMNEY, MOLLY'S IN SOULARD

SERVES 6

4 ounces brown sugar

4 ounces chili powder

4 ounces bacon

1/2 cup butter

1 teaspoon kosher salt

14 ounces marshmallows

2 ounces dark chocolate, chopped

2 tablespoons maple syrup

6 cups Rice Krispies

Preheat the oven to 350 degrees. In a bowl, combine the brown sugar and chili powder. Coat both sides of the bacon with the spice mixture, lay it on a sheet pan, and bake it for 8 to 10 minutes. Remove the bacon from the pan and place it on a paper towel to drain and cool. Once the bacon's cool, finely chop it.

Add the butter to a medium-size skillet over medium heat. Let it brown slightly. Add the kosher salt and marshmallows and cook until the marshmallows are just melted. Add the chocolate, bacon, maple syrup, and Rice Krispies. Thoroughly mix together all of the ingredients. Place the mixture on a baking sheet and press it down. Let it cool, then cut it into squares.

BERRY-MINT POPS

KAYLEN WISSINGER,

WHISK: A SUSTAINABLE BAKESHOP

SERVES 16

2 cups raspberries

2 cups blackberries

2 cups strawberries, sliced

1/4 cup lemon juice

1/4 cup fresh mint, finely minced

2/3 cup sugar

2/3 cup water

Combine the raspberries, blackberries, strawberries, lemon juice, and mint in a mixing bowl. Mash the berries a bit with the back of a large wooden spoon. Let the mixture sit for about 30 minutes to macerate. Meanwhile, combine the sugar and water in a small saucepan and simmer until the sugar is dissolved. Let the syrup cook for about 5 minutes, then combine it with the berry mixture.

Pour the berry mixture into popsicle molds. Freeze them, then enjoy.

BING-CHERRY CREPES

RHONDA CRANE,

MAGPIE'S RESTAURANT

MAKES 16 TO 20 CREPES

3 8-ounce packages cream cheese, softened

1/2 cup sugar or Splenda

1 lemon, juiced

1 teaspoon vanilla extract

1/2 teaspoon almond extract

16 to 20 crepes (homemade or available in

the grocery store in the frozen-food area)

Bing cherry sauce (see recipe)

Whipped cream

BING-CHERRY SAUCE

3 cans of dark sweet cherries with juice, not
in heavy syrup

3/4 cup sugar

2 tablespoons cornstarch

1/3 cup cold water

1/4 teaspoon salt

1/2 lemon, juiced

1/2 teaspoon almond extract

1 tablespoon butter, cut into pieces

Pour the cherries and their juices into a medium-size saucepan. Mix the sugar and cornstarch together, making sure to remove all the lumps. Add the cold water and mix well. Pour this syrup onto the cherries and bring the liquid to a boil over medium heat. Cook the sauce until it's thickened. Stirring constantly, continue to cook the sauce for another 3 minutes, then remove it from the heat. Mix in the salt, lemon juice, almond extract, and butter, stirring to melt all the butter.

With a mixer, mix the cream cheese until it's smooth and creamy. Then add the sugar, lemon, and extracts and beat them until they're well-mixed. Warm a crepe in a pan. Then place a crepe with the brownest side down, put filling on one side (for a 6-inch crepe, you'll need about 3 tablespoons of filling), and roll it up. Pour warm bing-cherry sauce over the cheese-filled crepes and top them with whipped cream.

CHOCOLATE LAYERED DESSERT

TONY ALMOND,
ALMONDS RESTAURANT

SERVES 12

1 stick margarine

1 1/4 cup flour

1/2 cup pecans, chopped, plus extra

1/2 cup powdered sugar

8 ounces cream cheese

1 8-ounce container Cool Whip

2 packages chocolate-pudding mix

3 cups milk

Preheat the oven to 375 degrees. Cut the margarine into the flour. Mix to combine them, then add 1/2 cup chopped pecans. Pat the dough into a lightly greased 9- by 13-inch baking pan. Bake the crust for 20 minutes, remove it from the oven, and let it cool.

Mix the powdered sugar with the cream cheese and half of the Cool Whip. Spread the mixture over the cooled crust. Chill it for 1 hour.

In a saucepan, combine the pudding mix and milk and cook it until it's thick. Let the pudding cool, then spread it over the cream cheese–and–Cool Whip mixture. Spread the remaining Cool Whip over the pudding. Sprinkle the top with chopped pecans. Chill the dessert and keep it in the refrigerator until you're ready to serve it.

Chocolate Chiffon Tart

CARL McCONNELL, STONE SOUP COTTAGE

SERVES 4

½ cup dark chocolate,
   broken up
1 cup water
3 egg yolks
1 teaspoon gelatin
¼ cup water
3 egg whites
¾ cup sugar
4 tart shells
Whipped cream
Fresh fruit

Combine the chocolate and water in a saucepot over low heat. Bring it to a slow simmer, stirring frequently until the water and chocolate are combined. Remove the liquid from the heat.

Whisk together the melted chocolate and the egg yolks until they're fully mixed. Place the pot back on low heat, stirring frequently until the mixture is thickened, 3 to 5 minutes. Remove the mixture from the heat and set it aside.

Sprinkle the gelatin over ¼ cup of water in a small saucepan. Heat the mixture over low heat until the gelatin dissolves. Whisk this into the chocolate mixture. Set this aside to cool at room temperature, about 2 hours. The mixture will thicken and start to set.

Whisk the egg whites and sugar to a stiff meringue. Combine the meringue and the chocolate mixture. Fill the tart shells and refrigerate them for 2 to 4 hours before serving. Garnish the tarts with whipped cream and fresh fruit and serve.

CHOCOLATE SOUFFLÉ

KEVIN TAYLOR, BISTRO 1130

SERVES 4

5 ounces bittersweet or semisweet chocolate

3 egg yolks

3 egg whites

1/3 cup sugar, plus extra for the ramekins

Butter

1/2 cup heavy cream

3 tablespoons powdered sugar

1 tablespoon Grand Marnier

Preheat the oven to 400 degrees. Fill a saucepan with water and bring it to a simmer. Melt the chocolate in a steel pan over the water. Remove the chocolate from the heat, add the egg yolks, and stir them in to thicken the mixture. In a bowl, whip the egg whites with the sugar to form stiff peaks. Gently fold the chocolate mixture into the egg whites.

Use butter to grease four ramekins, then sprinkle them with sugar. Carefully spoon the batter into the prepared ramekins. Bake the soufflés for 20 to 25 minutes, until the top has risen and is slightly cracked.

Use a stand mixer to whip the cream and powdered sugar into medium fluffy peaks. Mix in the Grand Marnier. Serve the whipped cream on top of each soufflé.

CREAMY POUND CAKE WITH STRAWBERRY-LEMON SAUCE

HELEN FLETCHER, THE ARDENT COOK AND TONY'S

SERVES 4

Nonstick baking spray

1 cup butter, room-temperature

3 cups sugar

6 eggs

1 tablespoon vanilla extract

1 cup cake flour

1 3/4 cups all-purpose flour

1/4 teaspoon salt

1 cup 40-percent cream

Strawberry-lemon sauce (see recipe)

Spray a tube pan very well with nonstick baking spray and set it aside.

Mix together the butter and sugar until it's light and fluffy. Add the eggs three at a time, beating the mixture well after each addition. Beat in the vanilla extract.

Sift the cake flour, all-purpose flour, and salt together. Add this to the batter alternately with the cream, starting and ending with flour. Pour the batter into the tube pan and smooth the top.

Place the pan in a cold oven. Set the oven to 275 degrees. Bake the cake for 1 hour and 15 minutes to 1 hour and 30 minutes, or until it's golden brown on top and a tester comes out clean. Let the cake cool for 15 to 20 minutes before releasing it from the pan.

Serve the cake with fresh strawberry-lemon sauce.

STRAWBERRY-LEMON SAUCE

4 cups strawberries, sliced

1 tablespoon lemon juice

½ lemon, zested

⅓ to ½ cup sugar

¼ teaspoon pepper (optional)

Combine the strawberries, lemon juice, lemon zest, sugar to taste, and optionally pepper in a mixing bowl, about an hour before serving. Let the sauce rest at room temperature.

Note: This is a fantastic, easy pound cake. The only caveat is to make sure the butter is really soft, or it won't blend together with the large amount of sugar. It is a dense cake, as pound cakes are, but it has a moistness and flavor that are unbelievable. It literally lasts for days under a cake cover and freezes well.

DARK-CHOCOLATE GALETTE WITH ROASTED RASPBERRIES, FRANGELICO, AND WHITE CHOCOLATE

STEPHEN TROUVERE, BAILEYS' CHOCOLATE BAR, BRIDGE, AND ROOSTER

SERVES 6

1 teaspoon lime juice

⅛ teaspoon salt

1 cup heavy cream

12 ounces bittersweet chocolate (60 to 75 percent cocoa), chopped

2 egg yolks

4 to 6 tablespoons Frangelico

1 pound puff pastry

1 egg yolk

1 tablespoon water

6 ounces raspberries

2 tablespoons sugar

1 bar best-quality white chocolate, chilled

½ cup hazelnuts, toasted and cracked

Preheat the oven to 375 degrees. In a pot, bring the cream, lime juice, and salt to a boil, then slowly pour it over the chocolate in a separate bowl and stir it until it's smooth. Let the mixture cool until it's tepid. Then whisk in the egg yolks and 2 to 4 tablespoons of the Frangelico. Chill this filling until it's firm, then scoop and mold about 3 tablespoons of the filling into a little disk. Repeat to create six disks.

On a lightly floured board, roll out the puff pastry and cut it into six squares measuring 5 inches per side. Pierce the center of each square with the tines of a fork, covering ⅓ of the total area with holes.

Mix 1 egg yolk with 1 tablespoon of water to form an egg wash. Brush the outside edges of the pastry with the wash and fold it up over the filling, leaving a gap so the filling remains visible. Crimp the seams gently, then egg-wash the remainder of the top of the pastry.

Place the galettes on a parchment-lined cookie sheet and chill them in the refrigerator for 10 to 15 minutes for best results. Then bake them until they're puffed and golden, 12 to 16 minutes.

While the galettes are baking, toss the raspberries with the sugar and 2 tablespoons of the Frangelico. Transfer the berries to a pie plate or small baking dish and roast them in the oven until the juices just begin to release from the berries. Remove the roasted berries from the oven.

Top each warm galette with a spoonful of the fruit and a few slivers of the white-chocolate bar, shaved with a vegetable peeler. Garnish the dessert with the toasted hazelnuts and serve it warm.

Key Lime Pie

FRAZER CAMERON, FRAZER'S RESTAURANT & LOUNGE

SERVES 6

---

1 ⅓ cup graham-cracker crumbs

½ cup unsalted butter, melted

3 large egg yolks

½ cup key-lime juice

1 14-ounce can sweetened condensed milk

1 ½ cups heavy cream

2 teaspoons sugar

¼ teaspoon vanilla extract

1 fresh lime, sliced

Moisten the graham-cracker crumbs with enough melted butter to keep them glued firmly together when squeezed in your palm. With the back of a tablespoon, press the crumbs into a 9-inch pie pan to form an even shell. Begin by pressing the crumbs into the side of the pan with the back of the spoon. Rest the thumb of your free hand on the rim of the pan. As you move the crumbs up the side of the pan with the spoon, use your thumb to press down and against the back of the spoon to form a tight, even edge about ½ inch thick. Continue around the entire side of the pan, then fill in the middle with the remaining crumbs.

Parbake the finished shell in a 350-degree oven for about 10 minutes. Midway, be sure the shell is not overbrowning. If so, remove it and cool.

In a stainless-steel or glass bowl, thoroughly mix the egg yolks with the lime juice and the sweetened condensed milk. Pour this mixture into the prepared pie shell and bake it at 350 degrees (reduce the oven's temperature to 300 if your shell baked too quickly at 350 degrees) for about 10 minutes, or until the custard is just set. Remove the pie from the oven and let it cool. Place it into the refrigerator until you're ready to serve it.

To make whipped cream, beat the cream by hand with a wire whip in a chilled stainless-steel or glass bowl, or use an electric mixer set at high speed. When soft peaks begin to form, add the sugar and vanilla extract. Continue beating the cream until the peaks become firm and fluffy, but not dry. Cover and refrigerate it until you're ready to use it.

Just before serving the chilled pie, spoon whipped cream onto its surface. Spread the whipped cream evenly from the center of the pie out to the edges. Slice the pie into six or seven pieces, garnish it with a slice of fresh lime, and serve it immediately.

EASY-PEASY HOT FUDGE SAUCE

ISABEL BIESTERFELD, JENNIFER'S
PHARMACY & SODA SHOPPE

SERVES 8

½ cup sugar

3 tablespoons cocoa powder

1 ½ tablespoons cornstarch

Salt

½ cup water, room-temperature

2 tablespoons butter

1 teaspoon pure vanilla extract

Mix the sugar, cocoa powder, cornstarch, and a dash of salt together in a 1-quart casserole or 2-cup glass measuring cup. Stir in the water. Cook the mixture in the microwave on full power for 1 ½ minutes, stirring halfway through the cooking time. Stir in the butter. Cook the sauce on full power for 1 minute more, or until the butter is melted, stirring halfway through the cooking time. Thoroughly stir in the vanilla extract. Use the sauce immediately, or store it in the refrigerator for later use.

GRAND MARNIER CHOCOLATE MOUSSE

PAUL GABRIELE, AGOSTINO'S ITALIAN
RESTAURANT & BAR

SERVES 4

1 pound semisweet chocolate, cut into small
   pieces

2 tablespoons salted butter

½ cup granulated sugar, plus a pinch

6 egg yolks

6 tablespoons Grand Marnier

6 egg whites

1 cup heavy cream

2 tablespoons vanilla extract

½ cup espresso

Chocolate shavings

Whipped cream

Fresh strawberries

Bring about 1 inch of water to a simmer in a sauce-pan. Combine the chocolate, butter, and sugar in a heat-proof bowl and set the bowl over the simmering water. Let stand without stirring until the chocolate has melted. Remove bowl from heat and stir in egg yolks. Then add the Grand Marnier and espresso.

Beat the egg whites and a pinch of sugar to make an Italian meringue. Set aside.

Beat the heavy cream until it is really thick.

Using a wooden spoon, gently fold the egg whites and cream mixture into the melted chocolate–Grand Marnier mix.

Chill for at least 60 minutes. Serve in your favorite dessert glass and garnish with chocolate shavings, whipped cream, and fresh strawberries.

GRAND MARNIER SABAYON WITH FRESH BERRIES

BRYAN CARR, POMME CAFÉ,
POMME RESTAURANT, AND
ATLAS RESTAURANT

SERVES 8

1 ¼ cups whipping cream

½ cup sugar

Ice

5 egg yolks

1 orange, zested

¼ cup Grand Marnier

Hot water

Fresh berries

Cake or cookies

Whip the cream with ¼ cup of the sugar until stiff peaks form and set it aside. Prepare a large bowl half-filled with ice. In a separate large stainless-steel mixing bowl, combine the egg yolks, the other ¼ cup sugar, the orange zest, and the Grand Marnier.

Put a few inches of hot water in a large pot and place it on a stove over a low-medium flame. Place the bowl containing the egg mixture over the pot and whisk it constantly as it cooks. Continue until the whisk leaves trails in the mixture. Remove the bowl from the heat and set it in the bowl of ice. Stir the mixture until it's cold, fold in the whipped cream, then chill it thoroughly.

To serve the sabayon, spoon it into bowls and serve it with fresh berries and cake or cookies.

GRENOBLE WALNUT TARTS

JOHN SCHREINER, CAFÉ PROVENCAL

SERVES 12

2 pounds dark brown sugar

½ pound unsalted butter

8 eggs

4 cups walnuts, chopped

6 tablespoons heavy cream

2 tablespoons vanilla extract

Sweet pie pastry, frozen or made fresh, enough for two pies

Serendipity French vanilla ice cream

Preheat the oven to 325 degrees. In a double boiler, melt together the sugar and butter. With a wire whisk, stir in the eggs and cook the mixture until all the grainy texture is gone. It should feel silky-smooth and glisten.

Add the chopped walnuts and continue to cook the mixture over low heat in the double boiler to develop a strong walnut flavor.

Add the cream and vanilla extract. Cook the mixture for 10 minutes more, then pour it into two 1- by 8-inch tart shells that have been lined with the pie dough. Bake the tarts for 30 to 45 minutes, or until the mixture is set and the crust is light brown.

Serve the tarts at room temperature. These taste best the day they're made, but they'll last three days in a re-frigerator. If they're chilled, warm them very lightly over low heat before serving. Serve them with a scoop of French vanilla ice cream from Serendipity Homemade Ice Cream in Webster Groves.

GRILLED PEACH CRÈME BRÛLÉE

KELLY ENGLISH,
KELLY ENGLISH STEAKHOUSE

SERVES 10

2 cups heavy cream

1 small bunch fresh thyme, minced

1 Ugandan vanilla bean, split and scraped

⅔ cup sugar, plus extra for brûlée

5 egg yolks

6 peaches, halved and pitted

Salt

Thyme

4 tablespoons sugar

Spicy-and-sweet peach salsa *fresca* (see recipe)

Whipped cream

In a saucepan, combine the cream, thyme, vanilla bean, and half of the sugar. Place the liquid over medium heat and cook it until it bubbles around the edges of the pot. Separately, place the egg yolks and the other half of the sugar into a bowl and whisk them together.

Once the liquid in the saucepan is hot, slowly and steadily pour it into the egg-yolk mixture while whisking continuously. Quickly strain the mixture into a cool container.

Preheat the oven to 275 degrees. Separately, season the peach slices to taste with salt, thyme, and sugar. Grill them with the cut side down. Add the grilled peaches to a pan and pour the crème brûlée mixture on top. Bake the dessert for approximately 20 minutes, then chill it.

Before serving, sprinkle sugar on top of the custard and burn it with a torch. Serve the crème brûlée with peach-and-cilantro salsa *fresca* and fresh whipped cream.

SPICY-AND-SWEET SALSA *FRESCA*

MAKES APPROXIMATELY 1 ½ CUPS

- 8 peaches, washed, pitted, peeled, and diced small
- 2 jalapeños, roasted, peeled, seeded, and minced
- ½ teaspoon *sambal oelek* chili paste
- ¼ cup sugar
- 2 limes, juiced and zested
- 2 tablespoons rice-wine vinegar
- 20 cilantro leaves, cut into a chiffonade
- 10 mint leaves, cut into a chiffonade
- Salt

Mix together the peaches, jalapeños, *sambal oelek*, sugar, lime juice and zest, rice-wine vinegar, cilantro leaves, mint leaves, and salt to taste in a bowl and let the salsa sit for 1 hour before serving.

HONEY-POACHED FIGS WITH GORGONZOLA

VINCE BOMMARITO JR., TONY'S

SERVES 5

- 1 cup honey
- 1 cup white wine
- 1 cinnamon stick
- 1 tablespoon dried lavender
- 10 figs
- 1 package Gorgonzola cheese
- Warm bread

In a small saucepan, bring the honey, white wine, cinnamon stick, and lavender to a simmer.

Add the figs to the pan one by one. Poach the figs for 2 to 3 minutes. The figs should still be firm. Remove them with a slotted spoon. Reduce the liquid by half, strain out the lavender and cinnamon stick, and reserve the liquid.

Cut the figs in half crosswise. Place the bottoms on an oven-safe pan and place a small piece of Gorgonzola cheese on top of each. Then place the pan under the broiler to melt the cheese slightly. Replace the tops of the figs.

Divide the figs onto five plates and drizzle them with the reserved honey sauce.

Serve them with warm bread as a cheese-fruit course after dinner.

ITALIAN NUTELLA– AND–FRESH STRAWBERRY NO-BAKE CHEESECAKE

MARTIN LOPEZ, PICCIONE PASTRY

SERVES 18

Strawberry topping (see recipe)

Graham cracker–Nutella crust

Cheesecake (see recipe)

Strawberries

STRAWBERRY TOPPING

1 pound fresh or frozen strawberries, washed and stemmed

1/4 cup sugar

1/2 vanilla bean, split lengthwise

2 tablespoons water

1 envelope unflavored gelatin

2 tablespoons cold water

Add the strawberries, sugar, half vanilla bean, and water to a saucepan. Cook the mixture over medium heat until the strawberries are quite soft. Remove the vanilla bean. Use an immersion blender to purée the fruit. (You can also pour the strawberries into a regular blender, then return them to the pot to finish cooking.) Sprinkle the gelatin over the cold water in a small bowl. Allow it to sit for 1 to 2 minutes. Add the gelatin to the strawberry purée and gently cook them together over low heat.

CHEESECAKE

1 pound cream cheese, softened

1/2 cup powdered sugar

1 teaspoon vanilla extract

1 1/4 cups strawberry topping (see recipe)

1/2 cup heavy cream

In a stand mixer, using the paddle attachment, beat the cream cheese and powdered sugar on medium-low speed until smooth. Add the vanilla extract. Add 1/2 cup of the strawberry topping and reserve the remaining 3/4 cup.

In a separate bowl, whip the heavy cream into medium peaks. Fold the whipped cream into the strawberry-cheesecake batter. Continue gently folding until they're just combined.

GRAHAM CRACKER–NUTELLA CRUST

7 whole graham crackers

4 tablespoons unsalted butter, melted

2 tablespoons Nutella

2 tablespoons brown sugar

2 tablespoons cocoa powder

Salt

In a food processor, grind the graham crackers until they are broken into a fine powder. Add the butter, Nutella, brown sugar, cocoa powder, and a pinch of salt. Then process the mixture until all of the ingredients are well-incorporated. You may have to scrape down the sides of the bowl a few times. Press the crust evenly into the bottom and sides of an 8- or 9-inch springform pan.

To complete: Pour the cheesecake batter into the prepared graham cracker–Nutella crust. Tap the pan gently on the counter to bring any air bubbles to the surface. Let the cheesecake sit, uncovered, in the refrigerator for about 2 hours, or until it's set to the touch.

Once the cheesecake is set, pour the remaining 3/4 cup of strawberry topping over it. If the topping has set up in the pot, gently heat it for a minute, just until it's pourable.

Place the cheesecake back into the refrigerator and allow it to set, uncovered, for another 30 minutes, or until the topping is set. At this point, it is ready to serve, or you can cover it with plastic wrap and let it sit in the refrigerator for up to 24 hours.

Before unlocking the springform pan, run a knife around the edge of the cheesecake to loosen it. Top the dessert with the fresh strawberries and serve it cold.

LEMON-CURD CHEESECAKE BROWNIE

REX HALE, BASSO, THE MARKET AT THE CHESHIRE, THE RESTAURANT AT THE CHESHIRE, AND THREE SIXTY

SERVES 12

Nonstick baking spray

1 cup all-purpose unbleached flour

1 teaspoon baking powder

1/2 teaspoon salt

1 cup butter

1 cup sugar

1 teaspoon vanilla extract

1 egg

2 cups lemon curd

12 ounces cream cheese, room-temperature

15 ounces powdered sugar

2 limes, zested

3 eggs

Preheat the oven to 325 degrees. Spray a half-hotel pan with nonstick baking spray. Sift together the flour, baking powder, and salt. Separately, mix together the butter and sugar until it's light and creamy. Add the vanilla and 1 egg and mix just until they're incorporated. Then fold in the flour mixture. Spread the batter evenly on the bottom of the pan. Refrigerate the pan until this base is firm, then spread the lemon curd on top of it.

To make the cheesecake topping, mix the cream cheese in a stand mixer with a paddle attachment until it's smooth and creamy. Mix in the powdered sugar until no lumps appear. Add the lime zest and 3 eggs. Mix the batter until it's smooth, then pour it on top of the lemon curd. Bake the brownies for 1 hour.

LEMON SEMIFREDDO

JIM FIALA AND MATT ABESHOUSE, THE CROSSING

SERVES 6

1 cup fresh-squeezed lemon juice

1 1/2 cups sugar

6 egg yolks

2 eggs

10 tablespoons unsalted butter

1 cup heavy cream

1/4 cup powdered sugar

Place the lemon juice, sugar, egg yolks, eggs, and butter in a nonreactive saucepan. Whisk continuously over medium heat until the mixture is thick enough to coat the back of a spoon, about 20 minutes. Do not stop whisking, or the eggs will scramble. Once the lemon curd has thickened, place it in a container and put it in an ice bath to cool completely.

While the curd is cooling, whip the cream and powdered sugar to medium peaks in a stand mixer with a whisk attachment. Once the curd is cool, fold the whipped cream into it in batches. Pour the mixture into separate ramekins and freeze it for 24 hours before serving it.

LIMONCELLO– STRAWBERRY MOUSSE

BOB COLOSIMO,
ELEVEN ELEVEN MISSISSIPPI

SERVES 6 TO 8

1 tablespoon plain gelatin powder

1/3 cup boiling water

1/3 cup lemon juice

1/2 cup limoncello

1 lemon, zested

4 eggs

1 cup sugar

12 ounces mascarpone

1 pint fresh strawberries, cleaned and sliced

Dissolve the gelatin in the boiling water. Mix in the lemon juice, limoncello, and lemon zest. Separately, whip the eggs and sugar together until they're light and fluffy. Add the gelatin mixture and mascarpone. Whip the ingredients together until they're well combined.

Place a layer of strawberries in a serving bowl or cup. Spoon a layer of mousse over the strawberries. Repeat layers to the top of the cup, finishing with the mousse on top. Chill the mousse at least 1 hour, or up to 24 hours. Garnish each cup with a fresh strawberry.

MARSHMALLOWS

RUSSELL PING,
RUSSELL'S CAFÉ & BAKERY AND
RUSSELL'S ON MACKLIND

MAKES 12 MARSHMALLOWS

1/2 cup sugar

1 cup corn syrup

Salt

1 cup water

2 packets unflavored gelatin

1 teaspoon vanilla extract

Powdered sugar

Candy sticks

Dark chocolate and sprinkles, toasted coconut, or crushed peppermint

Combine the sugar, the corn syrup, a pinch of salt, and 1/2 cup of the water in a saucepan. Heat the mixture slowly over medium heat to prevent the sugar from burning.

While the sugar mixture is heating, combine the gelatin and the other 1/2 cup of water in the bottom of a stand-mixer bowl. The gelatin will need about 5 minutes to bloom in the water.

When the sugar mixture begins to boil and reaches 220 degrees on a candy thermometer, remove it from the heat. Quickly and carefully pour the hot sugar mixture into the mixer with the gelatin.

Using the whip attachment, start the mixer slowly to prevent the hot sugar from splashing (hot sugar in your face is not pleasant). Then turn the mixer to high and whip the sugar mixture for about 3 minutes.

With the mixer running, add the vanilla extract. Continue to whip until the marshmallow is bright white and fluffy, about 5 to 8 minutes. When the marshmallow is finished, you will need to work quickly. Scrape it into a large piping bag, and pipe it into small plastic cups that have been coated with powdered sugar. Place candy sticks into the marshmallows. They will need to dry out for a few hours before you can unmold them.

Unmold the marshmallows and dip them in something delicious, like dark chocolate and candy sprinkles, toasted coconut, or crushed peppermint.

CHRISTY AUGUSTIN, PINT SIZE BAKERY

Augustin and her husband took a much-needed vacation to New York City after opening the bakery in 2012 and found that nearly every restaurant in town was serving house-made ricotta—either as an appetizer with honey, olive oil, and toasted artisan bread or as an ingredient in a pasta dish. They returned home determined to make their own. Realizing how easy and delicious it could be, Augustin and her bakers knew they had to find a use for it. She did—in a cake.

Orange-Ricotta Bundt Cake

CHRISTY AUGUSTIN, PINT SIZE BAKERY

MAKES 1 STANDARD BUNDT CAKE OR 9- BY 5-INCH LOAF

Nonstick baking spray

³/₄ cup unsalted butter, room-temperature

1 ½ cups plus 1 tablespoon granulated sugar

1 teaspoon kosher salt

1 orange, zested

1 ½ cups homemade ricotta cheese (see recipe)

3 large eggs, room-temperature

1 teaspoon pure vanilla extract

2 tablespoons triple sec, Grand Marnier, or Cointreau

1 ½ cups cake flour

2 ½ teaspoons baking powder

Powdered sugar or orange marmalade (optional)

HOMEMADE RICOTTA CHEESE

MAKES APPROXIMATELY 1 ½ CUPS

4 cups whole milk

2 cups heavy cream

1 teaspoon kosher salt

3 tablespoons cider vinegar

HOMEMADE RICOTTA CHEESE

Moisten two layers of cheesecloth and then use them to line a fine mesh strainer set over a large bowl. Make sure that the strainer's edge rests on the edge of the bowl and that the bottom of the strainer is at least 2 inches above the bottom of the bowl. Combine the milk, cream, and salt in a heavy-bottomed stainless-steel pot and bring the mixture to a simmer over medium-high heat. Just before it boils, turn off the heat and add the vinegar, stirring gently for 10 to 15 seconds. Allow the mixture to stand for up to 1 minute, until you begin to see the curd forming. It will separate into thicker curd and milky whey. Carefully pour the separated mixture into the strainer and let it sit, without stirring, for 10 to 15 minutes. The whey will drain off of the curd (the ricotta cheese). Chill the ricotta for at least 12 hours before using.

Preheat the oven to 365 degrees. Use nonstick baking spray to coat a bundt or loaf pan (even if it has a nonstick surface).

Using a stand mixer with a paddle attachment, mix together the butter, sugar, kosher salt, and orange zest on medium speed until it's light and fluffy. Scrape the bowl well using a rubber spatula, add the ricotta cheese, and mix again until everything is well-incorporated. Add the eggs one at a time, scraping well after each. Add the vanilla and the orange liqueur with the mixer still running, but on a lower speed to avoid a mess.

Sift together the cake flour and baking powder. Add this mixture into the bowl slowly, on the lowest speed. Stop and scrape down the bowl halfway through mixing and again when finished. Do not overmix.

Pour the finished batter into the sprayed pan and bake it for 45 minutes to 1 hour. The cake will pull away slightly from the edges of the pan and spring back in the center when gently touched. Let the cake cool in the pan for 5 to 10 minutes, or until it is cold to the touch, before unmolding it.

To unmold the cake, place a plate on top of the pan. Holding onto the edge of the pan, flip it over and set it down on the plate. If the cake is still warm, it should come right out. Serve it at room temperature dusted with powdered sugar or with orange marmalade poured over the top before slicing.

PEANUT-BUTTER
KIT KAT

MATHEW UNGER,
MATHEW'S KITCHEN

SERVES 16

GANACHE

    2 pounds semisweet chocolate chips

    2 cups heavy cream

    1/4 cup butter

Place the chocolate chips into a small bowl. In a sauce-pan, slowly bring the heavy cream to a boil. Add the butter. Pour the liquid into the bowl of chocolate and fold it with a spatula until the chocolate melts.

PEANUT-BUTTER MIXTURE

    Water

    5 pounds peanut butter

    1 pound butter

    2 cups powdered sugar

    3 cups rice cereal

Bring a pan of water to a simmer. In a stainless-steel bowl over the simmering water, melt the peanut butter and butter together. Whisk in the powdered sugar, then fold in the rice cereal until you have an even consistency.

To complete: Line a 9- by 9-inch pan with parchment paper. Keep the ganache and the peanut-butter mixture warm over a double boiler so that they will pour and spread easily. Pour a layer of ganache into the pan and let it cool in the refrigerator before adding a layer of the peanut-butter mixture. Alternate layers, cooling the pan after each. When all the layers have been poured, chill the dessert completely. Flip the dessert onto a cutting board, slice it, and serve it.

PEAR TARTE
TATIN WITH
PÂTÉ SABLÉE

CHRIS LEE,
RIVER CITY CASINO

SERVES 8

PÂTÉ SABLÉE PASTRY ROUNDS

MAKES 2 ROUNDS

    1 1/4 cups all-purpose flour

    1 1/4 cups powdered sugar

    1/2 cup finely ground almonds

    1/4 teaspoon salt

    1/2 cup cold butter

    1 egg

In a small bowl, mix together the flour, sugar, ground almonds, and salt.

Using a pastry cutter, a large-tined fork, or a food processor on the pulse setting, cut the cold butter into the flour until it resembles coarse sand with a few pea-size pieces of butter still visible.

Stir the egg into the mixture and toss it gently a few times, just until it forms a ball that holds together.

Separate the dough into two balls, flatten them slightly into thick disk shapes, wrap them in plastic wrap, and chill them for several hours before rolling them out.

When you're ready to use the dough, place a piece of plastic wrap on a work surface.

Unwrap the dough, place it on the plastic wrap, cover it with another piece of plastic wrap, and gently roll it into a 10-inch circle, lifting the plastic as needed to avoid sticking.

PEAR TARTE TATIN

- ¹/₂ cup sugar
- 1 ¹/₂ teaspoons cider vinegar
- 2 tablespoons water
- 2 tablespoons unsalted butter
- 3 Anjou or Bartlett pears, peeled, cored, and cut into six wedges each
- 1 chilled pâté sablée pastry round (see recipe)

In a medium cast-iron or ovenproof nonstick skillet, combine the sugar, vinegar, and 2 tablespoons water.

Cook the syrup over medium heat, without stirring, until it's golden, or 12 to 15 minutes. Stir in the butter. Arrange the pear wedges in a circle along the edge of the skillet. Reduce the heat to medium-low, and cook the pears until they're crisp-tender, 10 to 15 minutes. Remove the skillet from the heat.

Preheat the oven to 375 degrees. Drape the chilled pastry round over the pears, tucking the edge under. Place a small oven-safe plate or pot lid on top of the pastry and bake it for 15 minutes. Remove the plate and continue to bake the tart until the pastry is golden brown, about 15 minutes more. Let the tart cool in the skillet for 15 minutes. Run a knife around the edge of the skillet, carefully invert the tart onto a serving plate, and serve it warm.

PINEAPPLE UPSIDE DOWN CAKE
COLLEEN THOMPSON, CAIFE CAIFE AND COLLEEN'S COOKIES

- 1 ¹/₂ tablespoon unsalted butter
- 1 cup brown sugar
- 1 can pineapple circles, drained
- ¹/₂ cup golden raisins (optional)
- ¹/₂ cup chopped walnuts (optional)
- 1 ³/₄ cups all-purpose flour
- ¹/₂ teaspoon baking soda
- 1 teaspoon baking powder
- 1 teaspoon dry ginger (or 2 teaspoons fresh ginger, chopped)
- 1 teaspoon cinnamon
- ¹/₄ teaspoon cloves
- ¹/₄ teaspoon nutmeg
- ¹/₂ teaspoon salt
- 3 tablespoons shortening
- ¹/₂ cup granulated sugar
- 1 large egg
- ¹/₂ cup molasses
- ¹/₂ cup boiling water

Preheat the oven to 350 degrees. In a hot, 12-inch cast-iron skillet, melt butter and brown sugar. Heat it until it's just beginning to boil. Remove from the heat. Add the drained pineapple circles to the bottom of the skillet. The spaces may be filled with golden raisins and chopped walnuts.

Sift the flour, baking soda, baking powder, ginger, cinnamon, cloves, nutmeg, and salt.

Cream the shortening and sugar. Add the egg and molasses. Add the dry ingredients to the molasses mixture. Add the ¹/₂ cup of boiling water and mix well.

Pour the batter over the pineapple slices in the skillet. Bake the cake at 350 degrees for 25 to 30 minutes.

RUBY

NATHANIEL REID,
THE RITZ-CARLTON, ST. LOUIS

SERVES 8

Raspberry-tea chocolate mousse (see recipe)

6 ounces fresh raspberries

Tender chocolate cake (see recipe)

RASPBERRY-TEA CHOCOLATE MOUSSE

1/2 cup plus 1 tablespoon plus 1 teaspoon whole milk

1 tablespoon raspberry tea leaves

5/8 teaspoon powdered gelatin

1 tablespoon cold water

4 ounces 66-percent dark chocolate, finely chopped

1 tablespoon plus 2 teaspoons granulated sugar

1 cup whipping cream

Bring the whole milk to a boil, then add the raspberry tea to it and let it infuse for 5 minutes. Strain the milk with a fine strainer and press hard on the tea to extract the most flavor.

Sprinkle the gelatin powder over the cold water. Pour the warm milk infusion over the chocolate and whisk in the gelatin-and-water mixture. Let the mixture sit for 3 to 4 minutes, then stir it until it's smooth and shiny. Let the mixture cool to 86 degrees.

Add the sugar to the cream and whip the cream until it forms soft peaks. Fold the whipped cream into the chocolate.

TENDER CHOCOLATE CAKE

3 1/2 ounces 66-percent dark chocolate

4 tablespoons unsalted butter

3 egg whites

1/4 cup plus 1/2 teaspoon granulated sugar

3 egg yolks, beaten

2 tablespoons plus 1 teaspoon all-purpose flour

In a double boiler, melt the chocolate and butter together to approximately 130 degrees.

Whip the egg whites to medium peaks and slowly whip in the sugar. Fold half of this meringue mixture into the melted chocolate and butter. Fold in the beaten egg yolks, then fold in the remaining meringue delicately. Sift the flour and delicately fold it into the chocolate.

Preheat the oven to 375 degrees. Using a spatula, spread the cake batter 3/8 inch thick onto a sheet pan lined with parchment paper. Bake the cake for 10 to 14 minutes.

To complete: Place some of the raspberry-tea chocolate mousse into a mold or glass. Place a few raspberries on top. Cut out a piece of the soft chocolate cake and put it on top. If you're serving this dessert in a glass, the procedure can be repeated to make layers. Store the dessert in the refrigerator. Take it out of the refrigerator 10 minutes before serving.

S'MORES WITH HOMEMADE GRAHAM-CRACKER SHORTBREAD, MARSHMALLOW FLUFF, AND THE BEST CHOCOLATE SAUCE EVER

JOHN PERKINS, ENTRE

SERVES 4 TO 6

Graham-cracker shortbread (see recipe)

Marshmallow fluff (see recipe)

Best Chocolate Sauce Ever (see recipe)

GRAHAM-CRACKER SHORTBREAD

2 1/2 cups flour

1 cup packed dark brown sugar

1 teaspoon baking soda

3/4 teaspoon salt

7 tablespoons butter, cubed

1/3 cup molasses or honey

5 tablespoons milk

2 tablespoons vanilla extract

Mix the flour, brown sugar, baking soda, and salt in a food processor. Cut in the butter. Whisk together the molasses, milk, and vanilla separately, then add them slowly into the food processor and blend. Press the mixture into a tart or jellyroll pan and chill it for 1 hour in the refrigerator. Perforate the dough with a fork and bake it at 350 degrees until it's set, or 8 to 10 minutes. Remove the shortbread and let it cool, then cut it into 12 pieces.

MARSHMALLOW FLUFF

3 egg whites

2 cups light corn syrup

1/2 teaspoon kosher salt

2 cups powdered sugar

1 tablespoon vanilla extract

Combine the egg whites, corn syrup, and salt in the bowl of a standard mixer and mix on high until it doubles in volume. The mixture should be extremely thick. Turn the speed to low and mix in the powdered sugar and vanilla.

BEST CHOCOLATE SAUCE EVER

Adapted from Dessert FourPlay *by Johnny Iuzzini and Roy Finamore*

1 cup water

3/4 cup sugar

3/4 cup unsweetened cocoa

1/2 cup heavy cream

1/2 teaspoon Colgin liquid smoke

Combine the sugar and water in a saucepan. Heat and stir the liquid until the sugar is dissolved. Pour the cocoa into a bowl and whisk in the syrup until it's smooth. Return the mixture to the saucepan and bring it to a boil. Add the cream. Lower the heat to a simmer and stir the liquid frequently for about 30 minutes. Add the liquid smoke to taste.

To assemble the s'mores, spread marshmallow fluff between two pieces of the graham-cracker shortbread. Serve the chocolate sauce in a shooter glass alongside the plate.

STRAWBERRIES AND PANNA COTTA

KEVIN NASHAN,
SIDNEY STREET CAFE

SERVES 8

4 sheets silver-grade gelatin (available at
Kitchen Conservatory)

Ice water

1 cup white chocolate, chopped

1 ^{3}/$_4$ cups heavy cream

2 tablespoons sugar

1 ^{3}/$_4$ cups buttermilk

Vanilla-bean financiers (see recipe)

Macerated strawberries (see recipe)

Strawberry confit (see recipe)

Soak the gelatin in ice water until it's softened, then drain it and place it in a bowl with the white chocolate. In a saucepot, bring the cream and sugar to a boil. Once it's boiling, pour the cream over the white chocolate and gelatin. Whisk until the chocolate is melted, then stir in the buttermilk. Pour the panna-cotta mixture into eight ramekins and chill it until it sets.

VANILLA-BEAN FINANCIERS

^{1}/$_4$ cup all-purpose flour

^{1}/$_2$ cup almond flour

^{3}/$_4$ cup powdered sugar

Salt

3 large egg whites, beaten

^{1}/$_3$ cup butter, browned

1 vanilla bean, split, seeds scraped

Butter or nonstick baking spray

Preheat the oven to 400 degrees. Sift together the flour, almond flour, and powdered sugar. Add a pinch of salt.

Stir in the egg whites and mix until they're combined. Slowly add the brown butter and vanilla seeds and mix until they're combined. Bake the pastries in a greased mini muffin pan for 10 to 12 minutes, or until a tester inserted comes out clean.

MACERATED STRAWBERRIES

1 cup sugar

1 cup water

^{1}/$_2$ cup mint, chopped

1 pint strawberries, trimmed and sliced

Bring the sugar and water to a simmer over medium heat. Let the liquid simmer until the sugar is dissolved. Remove the syrup from the heat and add the mint. Chill the syrup, then pour it over the strawberries and let it set at least 1 hour.

STRAWBERRY CONFIT

1 pint strawberries, cleaned and halved

Sugar

Salt

Olive oil

Preheat the oven to 175 degrees. Toss the strawberries, sugar, salt, and olive oil to taste. Place the strawberries on a lined cookie sheet and roast them for about 3 hours, or until the berries are similar to sun-dried tomatoes. Add seasoning if necessary.

To complete: Top the panna cotta with the vanilla-bean financiers and strawberry confit. Serve this in a cereal bowl; for a party, Nashan suggests using a cocktail glass.

SUGAR COOKIES

TONY ALMOND,
ALMONDS RESTAURANT

MAKES 2 DOZEN

²/₃ cup shortening

³/₄ cup granulated sugar

1 teaspoon vanilla extract

1 egg

4 teaspoons milk

2 cups all-purpose flour

1 ½ teaspoons baking powder

¼ teaspoon salt

1 box powdered sugar

Butter or nonstick baking spray

3 ounces cream cheese, softened (optional)

2 tablespoons butter, softened (optional)

Milk (optional)

Preheat the oven to 350 degrees. Thoroughly mix together the shortening, granulated sugar, and vanilla extract until it's smooth and creamy. Add the egg and beat the mixture until it's light and fluffy. Stir in the milk.

In a separate bowl, mix together the flour, baking powder, salt, and powdered sugar, then blend it into the shortening mixture. On a lightly floured surface, roll out the cookie dough. Cut it into shapes. Lightly grease or spray a cookie sheet, place the cookies on it, and bake them until their edges are lightly browned, 8 to 10 minutes.

For the icing, which is optional, mix together the cream cheese and butter until it's smooth. Add just enough milk to thin the mixture. Ice the cookies.

WARM CHOCOLATE
SOUFFLÉ CAKE

REX HALE, BASSO, THE MARKET AT
THE CHESHIRE, THE RESTAURANT AT
THE CHESHIRE, AND THREE SIXTY

MAKES 10 CAKES

1 pound plus 6 ounces bittersweet chocolate

10 tablespoons butter

12 eggs

2 tablespoons Grand Marnier

3 tablespoons cornstarch

1 ½ cups sugar

Nonstick baking spray

Seasonal ice cream

Melt the chocolate and butter together. Separate the eggs and add the Grand Marnier, cornstarch, and half of the sugar to the egg yolks. Whisk the mixture until it's smooth. Whip the egg whites with the remaining half of the sugar until soft peaks are formed.

Preheat the oven to 350 degrees. Spray 3-inch stainless rings or cups with nonstick baking spray. Fold the chocolate-butter mixture into the egg-yolk mixture, then into the whipped egg whites. Spoon the final mixture into rings or cups and bake for 9 to 12 minutes, or until the cake is set on the outside but still soft in the center. Allow the cakes to cool for a couple of minutes. Serve each cake with seasonal ice cream.

Drinks

19TH CENTURY

TED KILGORE, PLANTER'S HOUSE

SERVES 1

1 ½ ounce Broker's gin

¾ ounce yellow chartreuse

¾ ounce Rothman & Winter Orchard Pear
   liqueur

¼ ounce white crème de cacao

½ lemon, juiced

Lemon rind

Combine all liquid ingredients and shake. Serve up with a lemon twist.

AN APPLE FAR FROM THE TREE

CHARLIE MYERS,
MCGURK'S PUBLIC HOUSE

SERVES 1

2 ounces Stoli Gala Applik vodka

1 ½ ounces Jim Beam Jacob's Ghost white
   whiskey

1 ½ ounces apricot brandy

1 ½ ounces Granny Smith apple juice

Lemon slice or cinnamon stick

Mix all liquid ingredients together in a mixing glass using a bar spoon. Strain the mixture into a martini or coupe glass. Garnish it with lemon in the spring and cinnamon in the fall.

BANGKOK FIZZ

JUSTIN CARDWELL, BC'S KITCHEN

SERVES 1

1 ounce Tanqueray gin

1 ounce Stone's Original Green ginger wine

1 ounce fresh lime juice

1 ounce lemongrass-thyme syrup (see recipe)

1 egg white

2 ounces cold club soda

Fresh thyme

LEMONGRASS-THYME SYRUP

2 cups sugar

1 cup water

½ cup fresh lemongrass

1 tablespoon fresh thyme, chopped

Combine the sugar and water in a pot and bring it to a boil. Pull the pot from the heat and add the lemongrass and thyme. Steep the herbs for 15 minutes, then strain out the solids. Bottle and chill the syrup.

Combine the gin, ginger wine, lime juice, lemongrass-thyme syrup, and egg white in a shaking tin and "dry shake" it without ice to combine it and froth the egg white. Add ice to the tin and shake it hard. Strain the drink into a chilled glass and top it with the cold club soda to fizz. Garnish it with a fresh thyme sprig.

BUMBOO PUNCH

JUSTIN CARDWELL, BC'S KITCHEN

SERVES 1

- 2 ounces añejo rum
- 1 ounce fresh grapefruit juice
- ½ ounce cinnamon syrup (see recipe)
- 1 tablespoon apricot jam
- 1 whole nutmeg

CINNAMON SYRUP

- 2 cups sugar
- 1 cup water
- 2 sticks cinnamon

Boil together the sugar and water in a pot. Remove the pot from the heat and add the cinnamon sticks. Let them steep for 15 minutes, then strain them out. Bottle and chill the syrup.

Combine the rum, grapefruit juice, cinnamon syrup, and apricot jam in a shaking tin and top it with ice. Shake to combine the ingredients. Strain the drink into a glass filled with crushed ice. (Regular ice can also be used, or you can even just pour the contents of the shaker straight into the serving glass.) Garnish it with a grating of fresh nutmeg over the top.

CHILL DAY

CHARLIE MYERS, MCGURK'S PUBLIC HOUSE

SERVES 1

- 2 ½ ounces cucumber-infused Purus vodka
- 2 dashes Fee Brothers mint bitters
- ½ ounce simple syrup
- 2 ounces club soda
- Fresh spearmint

Mix the cucumber-infused vodka, mint bitters, simple syrup, and club soda and strain it over crushed ice. Smack the sprig of mint to release the essential oils and place it as a garnish.

CUCUMBER COLLINS

BROOKSEY CARDWELL, BC'S KITCHEN

SERVES 1

- 5 mint leaves
- ½ lime, seeded and peeled
- 1 ½ ounces cucumber-infused vodka or
  Pearl cucumber vodka
- Ginger beer

Muddle the mint leaves and half lime and add the cucumber vodka. Pour the mixture over crushed ice in a Collins glass and top it with the ginger beer.

EL ÁNGEL ROJO

CHARLIE MYERS AND MEL JAMES, MCGURK'S PUBLIC HOUSE

SERVES 1

Salt and pepper

2 ounces strawberry-mint–infused
 1800 Reposado tequila

½ ounce simple syrup

1 ounce fresh lime juice

4 dashes Regans' Orange Bitters No. 6

2 ounces fresh strawberry purée

1 ounce Corona beer

Mint sprig

Rim a glass with an equal combination of salt and pepper. Add ice, and set it aside. Mix the strawberry-mint–infused tequila, simple syrup, lime juice, bitters, and strawberry purée in a shaking tin. Shake the mixture, then strain it over the ice in the rimmed glass, adding the Corona while pouring. Smack the mint to release its essential oils and place it in the glass as a garnish.

HIGH ON THE HOG MANHATTAN

KEYAN STILL, HENDRICKS BBQ

SERVES 1

2 ounces Willett bourbon

1 ounce house-smoked Cocchi Vermouth di
 Torino (see recipe)

1 bar spoon Heering cherry liqueur

2 dashes The Bitter Truth Old Time Aromatic
 Bitters

2 dashes The Bitter Truth Chocolate Bitters

Spiced, bourbon-soaked maraschino cherry

SMOKED COCCHI VERMOUTH DI TORINO

Take one bottle of Cocchi Vermouth di Torino and place it in a clean pot. Make a basket out of a mesh strainer to set on top of pot, with perforations on the sides to allow airflow. Take a smoldering chunk of applewood hickory and place it in the basket. Cover it with aluminum foil, but allow for the airflow to keep the smoke going. Smoke it for 30 to 45 minutes. You should not cook the Cocchi, only let the alcohol and smoke interact to soak up the smoky flavor. Store it in the original container with a label and date in refrigeration.

Combine the ingredients in a mixing glass. Add ice and stir for approximately 30 seconds, with variances for ice size and shape. Strain the drink into a chilled cocktail glass and garnish it with a spiced, bourbon-soaked maraschino cherry.

HIGHLAND COSMO

JUSTIN CARDWELL, BC'S KITCHEN

SERVES 1

1 ½ ounce Highland single-malt scotch

1 ounce Clear Creek Oregon cranberry
 liqueur

½ ounce lime juice

¼ ounce simple syrup

¼ ounce Cointreau

Orange rind

Excluding the orange rind, combine all ingredients with ice in a shaking tin. Shake it, then strain it into a martini glass. Garnish it with an orange twist.

LIVING IN BLY'S WORLD

BLAIR SCHRAUTEMEIER, CIELO

SERVES 1

³/₄ ounce cilantro-infused Hendrick's gin
   (see recipe)

³/₄ ounce avocado-and-jalapeño shrub (see
   recipe)

¹/₂ ounce lime juice

1 ounce champagne

CILANTRO-INFUSED HENDRICK'S GIN

1 ounce cilantro

1 bottle Hendrick's gin

Add the cilantro to the bottle of gin. Let it infuse for two hours, then strain it.

AVOCADO-AND-JALAPEÑO SHRUB

1 avocado, sliced

1 jalapeño, sliced

10 ounces (or ¹/₄ cup) champagne vinegar

2 ounces sugar

Cover the sliced avocado and jalapeño with vinegar for four days. Strain the mixture into a saucepan and add in the sugar. Boil it for 10 minutes and strain it. Allow the resulting liquid to cool.

Mix and serve.

NORI'S FAMOUS SANGRIA

**JORGE CALVO,
MANGO PERUVIAN CUISINE**

SERVES A CROWD

1 liter orange juice

1 liter well-reduced simple syrup

1 liter Rose's lime juice

1 liter premium citrus vodka

2 tablespoons ground cinnamon

4 bottles Spanish red wine (a cheap wine
   you'd still drink by itself)

Club soda

Apples and oranges, diced

Combine the orange juice, simple syrup, lime juice, citrus vodka, cinnamon, and red wine. Stir well. Serve the sangria over ice with a splash of club soda, as well as fresh diced apples and oranges.

PARIS (REVISITED)

NATE SELSOR, DEMUN OYSTER BAR

SERVES 1

1 ounce Aperol

1 ounce Cocchi Americano

3 ounces Cava (or any dry sparkling wine)

8 to 10 drops absinthe

Orange rind

Create this cocktail in a highball glass over ice and garnish it with a flamed orange twist.

PHILABUSTER

TED KILGORE, PLANTER'S HOUSE

SERVES 1

1 ½ ounce Rittenhouse rye

½ ounce Aperol

½ ounce Cocchi Americano

¼ ounce Cynar

⅛ ounce Fernet

1 dash Bittermens grapefruit bitters

Grapefruit rind

Combine all liquid ingredients and stir. Strain the mixture over a rock in a highball glass. Garnish the drink with a grapefruit twist.

SPAGHETTI WESTERN

TED KILGORE, PLANTER'S HOUSE

SERVES 1

1 ounce W.L. Weller 12-year-old bourbon

1 ounce Rittenhouse rye

¾ ounce Barolo Chinato

¼ ounce Averna amaro

1 dash Dr. Adam Elmegirab's Dandelion & Burdock Bitters

Grapefruit rind

Stir together all of the liquid ingredients. Serve the drink in a cocktail glass and garnish it with a grapefruit twist.

PRICKLY POMEGRANATE

AMANDA WILGUS, HERBIE'S VINTAGE 72

SERVES 1

Salt and pepper

8 to 10 arugula leaves

½ ounce agave nectar

1 ½ ounces Milagro tequila

1 ounce pomegranate juice

½ ounce lime juice

Rim a double rocks glass with salt and pepper and set it aside. Muddle the arugula leaves and agave nectar. Add the tequila, pomegranate juice, lime juice, and ice, and shake. Pour the mixture into the rimmed double rocks glass. Garnish it with an arugula leaf.

STRAWBERRY FIELDS

JUSTIN CARDWELL, BC'S KITCHEN

SERVES 1

1 ½ ounces strawberry gin (see recipe)

1 ounce St. Germain liqueur

1 ounce lemon juice

4 ounces club soda

1 strawberry

STRAWBERRY GIN

1 cup strawberries, chopped

1 bottle gin

Add the chopped strawberries to your favorite gin and let them infuse it for 2 to 4 days. Strain the gin before using it.

Combine the strawberry gin, St. Germain, and lemon juice in a serving glass. Top the liquid with ice and club soda, and stir it to combine. Garnish it with the strawberry.

SUBTLE HUSTLE

TED KILGORE, NICHE

SERVES 1

1 ounce Aperol

1 ounce Cocchi Americano

1/2 ounce lemon juice

1/2 ounce passion-fruit syrup

Brut champagne

The Bitter Truth Creole Bitters

Combine all ingredients, shake, and strain into a cocktail glass. Top with Brut and Creole Bitters.

THE BLOODY REVENGE

BROOKSEY CARDWELL, BC'S KITCHEN

SERVES 1

1 ounce Heaven Hill white-label bourbon

1 ounce Aperol

1 ounce blood-orange juice

1/2 ounce fresh lime juice

Lime wedge

Mix all the liquid ingredients and serve the drink in a martini glass with a wedge of lime.

THE GUILTY PLEASURE

BROOKSEY CARDWELL, BC'S KITCHEN

SERVES 1

Crushed pretzels

1 1/2 ounce DonQ Añejo rum

1/2 ounce The Big O ginger liqueur

1/2 ounce Cynar

1/4 ounce simple syrup

4 dashes Fee Brothers Aztec Chocolate bitters

Dark chocolate, shaved

Rim a martini glass with crushed pretzels and set it aside. Combine all the liquid ingredients, and serve them in the pretzel-rimmed martini glass, with a garnish of shaved dark chocolate.

**BROOKSEY
CARDWELL,
BC'S KITCHEN**

**What should every bar
have?** Fresh juices, bitters,
a quality rye whiskey, and
an Italian vermouth, like
Cocchi.

**What's your favorite
appliance?** Ice crusher

**Which bars do you
frequent?** Friendly's
in Tower Grove and
McGurk's Public House
in O'Fallon., Mo.

**Who taught you to mix a
drink?** My older brother,
Justin.

The Georgia Peach

BROOKSEY CARDWELL, BC'S KITCHEN

SERVES 1

1 ½ ounce peach-infused
Nolet's gin (see recipe)

1 ounce Dolin Blanco
vermouth

¼ ounce fresh lemon
juice

3 dashes peach bitters

1 peach, sliced into
wedges

PEACH-INFUSED NOLET'S GIN

1 ½ peaches, pitted and diced

1 bottle Nolet's gin

Cut the peach into bites and soak the fruit in the gin for 1 week.
Then strain the liquor to remove the peach.

In a shaking tin, shake the liquid ingredients. Serve the drink up in
a coupe glass, with a peach wedge.

THE LOLITA

JUSTIN CARDWELL, BC'S KITCHEN

SERVES 1

1 ½ ounces hibiscus-infused tequila (see recipe)

1 ½ ounces grapefruit syrup (see recipe)

4 ounces club soda

1 grapefruit, cut into wedges

HIBISCUS-INFUSED TEQUILA

1 bottle good-quality tequila blanco

1 tablespoon dried hibiscus flowers

Add the dried hibiscus flowers to the bottle of tequila and let it sit for 1 week, shaking it up every 2 days. Strain out the flowers and rebottle the tequila.

GRAPEFRUIT SYRUP

2 cups sugar

1 cup water

1 ruby grapefruit, zested and juiced

Bring the sugar and water to boil in a pot. Remove the pot from the heat and stir in the grapefruit juice and zest. Let it steep for 20 minutes, then strain the syrup through a fine mesh strainer. Bottle and chill the syrup.

Combine the liquid ingredients over ice and stir. Garnish the drink with a fresh grapefruit wedge.

THE SIBLING RIVALRY

BROOKSEY CARDWELL, BC'S KITCHEN

SERVES 1

1 ½ ounces Ketel One Oranje vodka

½ ounce crème de violette

½ ounce St. Germain liqueur

¼ ounce Domaine de Canton ginger liqueur

½ ounce lemon juice

Lemon rind

Shake together the liquid ingredients and pour the mixture into a martini glass. Serve the drink with a lemon twist.

TRÈS JOLIE

TOMMY GRAY, BAR LES FRÈRES

SERVES 1

2 ounces dry vermouth

1 ounce sweet vermouth

½ ounce Cointreau

2 dashes orange bitters

Orange rind

In a shaker, combine the liquors and bitters and shake over ice. Pour the drink into a chilled stemmed cocktail glass and garnish it with an orange twist.

WILLIE'S BREAKFAST

NICK LUEDDE, THE LIBERTINE

SERVES 1

Luedde was once told that Georgia peaches are Willie Nelson's favorite thing to eat in the morning. Luedde's favorite beverage on the planet is bourbon. So, he thought, "Breakfast for dinner? Sounds perfect." The bourbon and basil play together with a certain beauty, and Luedde added the dark spice of Angostura bitters to play nicely with the peaches. Wanting to add more balance, Luedde chose Campari for its bitter citrus notes. He recommends double-straining this, or at least using a fine mesh strainer.

³/₄ ounce lemon juice

4 basil leaves

1 ½ ounce Buffalo Trace bourbon

½ ounce Campari

2 dashes Angostura bitters

1 spoonful peach preserves

1 lemon twist

Add the fresh lemon juice and basil leaves to a rocks glass and softly muddle them. In a shaking tin, combine the Campari, bitters, and preserves and shake well. Strain the mix and serve it up. Finish the drink with a twist of lemon zest.

INDEX